D1461634

ABORTION AND THE SANCTITY
OF HUMAN LIFE

ABORTION
and the
SANCTITY OF HUMAN LIFE

Editor: J. H. Channer

Essays by

E. L. MASCALL   P. R. NORRIS
J. FOSTER   G. BONNER
G. B. BENTLEY   O. M. T. O'DONOVAN
J.W. ROGERSON   C. R. FRADD

Exeter
The Paternoster Press

AUSTRALIA:
Bookhouse Australia Ltd.,
P.O. Box 115, Flemington Markets, NSW 2129

SOUTH AFRICA
Oxford University Press,
P.O. Box 1141, Cape Town

British Library Cataloguing in Publication Data

Abortion and the sanctity of human life.
1. Abortion—Moral and ethical aspects
I. Channer, John Hugh
179'.76   HQ767.3

ISBN 0-85364-417-9

Typeset in Great Britain by
Busby's Typesetting & Design, 52 Queen Street, Exeter, Devon
and printed for The Paternoster Press,
Paternoster House, 3 Mount Radford Crescent, Exeter, Devon
by Cox & Wyman Ltd., Reading

Contents

The book has been edited by Hugh Channer, Vicar of St. Augustin's, Bournemouth.

Foreword

E. L. MASCALL

The most striking thing about the Abortion Act of 1967 is that it has entirely failed to fulfil the prophecies which were so confidently made by its proponents and which led many to give it their reluctant support even against their natural instincts. The emphatic assurance that was made that the Act neither intended nor, in fact, permitted abortion on demand has now been all but explicitly abandoned; in 1973 97 per cent of the women who went to one of the so-called "pregnancy advisory services" were given abortions, and it is significant that the advertisements for one of these agencies on the London Underground Railways are no longer headed "Pregnancy" but simply "Abortion". By 1975 nearly 90 per cent of the abortions in the private sector were done for the "mental health" of the mother and 99 per cent of these on grounds of neurosis and "transient situational disturbance". (The necessity of choosing between the life of the mother and that of the child, which had been the staple of the pro-abortionist argument, is becoming far less common under modern medical conditions; only three cases of saving the mother's life in an emergency by abortion were reported in England and Wales in 1983. 179, 148 operations were statutorily registered in 1983.)

Few of the abortions in the UK are the "hard cases" allegedly envisaged by the act; in 1983, 55 per cent of the British residents aborted had no children, and 86 per cent had no more than two.

Illegitimacy has not declined; from 1961 to 1981 the ratio of illegitimate to total live births in England and Wales rose from 6.0 to 12.8 per cent. Nor has criminal abortion come to an end. And the effects, both physical and psychological, on women who have had abortions have caused deep concern to the medical profession. Nevertheless, the number of legal abortions in this country shows no sign of decreasing and now totals well over two-million. Why, we might wonder, have the hopes so signally failed of achievement? The answer is fundamentally very simple; it is that abortion offers for many people a simple and rapid way out from a disagreeable situation, which may vary from something as trivial as the inability to take part in a sporting event to something as serious as the problem for an impoverished couple of supporting another member of an already underprivileged family. And for those whose ideal of a full and rewarding life is one centred in sexual promiscuity, abortion provides a longstop for the failed contraceptive.

Now it is not the primary purpose of this volume to offer alternative solutions to the problems, social and other, which abortion claims to meet. That purpose is to maintain that, whatever its advantages, real or apparent may be, abortion is immoral because it is the deliberate killing of an innocent and helpless human being; it is an attempt to solve human problems by the short cut of eliminating human beings. In the first three chapters of this book it is argued, on medical, philosophical and moral-theological grounds respectively, that a new human being comes into existence when a human ovum is fertilized by a human spermatozoon, that is to say with the unification of the genetic heritages of the two parents. As is shown by its capacity for division and development, the fertilized ovum has an inherent and active vitality that neither the unfertilized ovum nor the sperm alone possesses. It is for this reason that the description of abortion as "merely one kind of contraception" is quite inaccurate; there is all the difference in the world between preventing a human being from coming into existence and destroying one whose existence has already begun. The fact that the fertilized ovum is invisibly minute—only a tenth of a millimetre in dimension—is irrelevant except as a detail about the limitations of our eyesight; in that minute speck there is coded all the inherited physiological complexity of the adult human being. However, because of the tendency of our feeble imagination to collaborate with our unenlightened self-interest, there is a strong temptation to fix the becoming of the fetus "really human" at some later date: at the implantation of the fertilized ovum in the uterus (8 days); at the appearance of distinct organs and blood-circulation (30 days); at sleeping and response to stimuli (10 weeks); and so on, to birth after nine months. And experience shows that any attempt to fix an arbitrary date down to which abortion is allowable results in that date being progressively lowered, until the idea of killing a fully grown child even after birth becomes tolerable, provided some physical or mental defect renders it unattractive to its parents. However, for many people the imagination has more potent an influence than mere argument, and, as there seem still to be many people who salve their consciences by thinking of abortion as "simply removing a blob of jelly", it may be well to confront them with a photograph of the mangled remains of a fetus aborted by vacuum aspiration after ten weeks' gestation, with the limbs and ribs clearly visible. Nevertheless, the fact that we allow things to be done to a fetus which we would never allow to be done to a fully grown man or woman largely arises from the facts that the fetus is minute and unseen and unable to complain, all of which should be seen as totally irrelevant.

However, behind all this there is, I believe, a deeper issue, though a largely unrecognized one, namely the loss of any firm conviction of the inherent value of human nature. Our civilization grew up on the foundation of a belief in the essential dignity and nobility of man as such, a belief which was confirmed and elevated by the Christian proclamation that the Creator of the universe had himself become a man. That human beings, with a nature partly spiritual and partly material, were highly complicated creatures was frankly admitted. It would no doubt be much simpler to be a pure spirit or a pure animal, and if you were either an angel or a goat that was what you were meant to be; but to be a human being was to be something more complicated, more difficult and also more exciting. And in nothing was man more complicated than in that aspect of him that governed the propagation of his species. While on the one hand homogeneous with that which operated in any other of the higher mammals, in him it was intertwined with an intense and violent emotional life and subject to the judgment of a rational mind and will, whose ultimate satisfaction (the Christian would add) lay in union with the Creator himself. And, however much Christian and secularist might disagree about almost everything else, on this at least they were in accord, that human nature was ultimately meaningful and that therefore human happiness consisted in finding the truth about human nature and living in accordance with it. The matter is very different for those—and they are more and more common today—for whom human nature is not ultimately meaningful, who see mankind merely as a kind of foam thrown up by some amazingly improbable chance in the evolutionary flux, with no ultimate significance and no coherent unity, and for whom the intimate association between the propagation of the human species and the whole complex of emotional and erotic experience is a mere accident, to be explained, if at all, on grounds of evolutionary utility and survival value but having no real significance in itself. It is, I think, on these grounds that is to be explained one of the most disquieting phenomena of our time, namely the tendency to separate as far as possible the procreative and erotic functions of sex and to look for science to devise techniques for satisfying them in isolation from each other. There are, of course, immensely powerful interests behind this and they are largely independent of one another, though not less menacing in consequence. The commercial interests of the cosmetic and pornographic industries (soft and hard), the political pressures to remove education from the hands of parents into those of the state, the reluctance of geneticists and microbiologists to allow any constraints on their experiments with fertilized human ova, these and other tendencies in public life today, in spite of their diverse characters, agree in their tendency to make this separation. And the abortion movement is one manifestation of it. It is strengthened by the widespread demand for what has been described as "instant happiness". "The popular attitude today", writes the Bishop of London, "is that a person must be free to do what he wants, but that he must at the same time be freed from the consequences."[1] And again, Dr Leonard describes the present as "a time when happiness is equated with the avoidance of suffering and when anything is regarded as justified if it appears to enable suffering to be avoided".[2]

However, what we are concerned with in this book is abortion, though I do not think we can understand the present situation apart from its context. And it can be understood only as part of a widespread movement to view all moral issues from a purely subjective standpoint which has corroded the moral sense of many kindly and well disposed people. It is therefore important to stress that in opposing abortion we are not adopting a negative and repressive stance, but are making a positive defence of human rights. In the words of the United Nations Declaration of the Rights of the Child of 1959:

> The child, by reason of his physical and mental immaturity, needs special safeguards and care, including appropriate legal protection, before as well as after birth.

And, so far from it being true that abortionism is a defence of the rights of women, the precise opposite is true; it is treating the one thing that women can do and men cannot—bearing a child— as being a handicap and a disablement and not, as it is, their glory. Mary Kenny—herself a woman—writes:

> For most women, motherhood, however difficult the practical prospect of it may be, remains a greatly desired, and magically fulfilling, role. There are very often practical difficulties facing parents—almost always, one might say— but neither in the physiological organism nor in the emotional response is the normal relation between the womb and its fruit an adversarial one.
>
> Indeed, in denigrating the fruit of the womb, abortionism automatically carries with it a sub-conscious denigration of women, because it diminishes the feeling and the experience of woman in her act of creativity. ... It is hardly surprising that high-abortion societies are societies in which women have on the whole poor status and hard lives—Japan and the USSR being prime examples.[3]

In fact, far from "liberating" women, ready abortion gives power to all sorts of people to pressurize girls and women to take what is, for the pressurizer as much as for the pressurized, the easy way out; it can be, in the worst sense, an example of male chauvinism. It is unfortunately true that we live in a society whose public structure was mainly devised by men for men and in which women are able to compete successfully only at the cost of becoming themselves masculinized. And in such a situation the one feature which most notably distinguishes women from men is most easily the first to go. A really healthy society will not be one which offers women increased facilities for imitating men, but one which makes it easier and more natural for them to be themselves. It is plain that we have not achieved such a society either in the West or behind the Iron Curtain, but it is that for which genuine feminists should be working and not the bogus equalitarianism which seeks to assimilate women to men. And such a healthy society will not be one in which abortion is more readily available but one in which it has ceased to be asked for. For even if a pregnancy is the result of an immoral act there is nothing immoral in the birth to which it may lead and nothing shameful in the child who is born as a result of it. We should distinguish sharply between the act of fornication or adultery, which, is a matter for the Church's ministry of penitence and absolution, and the care and nurture of the child, who like every other child is a potential member of the Body of Christ. There is no place for the attitude of the censorious lady in Dickens's *Bleak House* expressed in the words, "Your mother was your shame, Esther, as you are hers", unless one is to suppose that guilt is a genetic mutation transmitted on one of the chromosomes. And this is perhaps a suitable place to end this Foreword, except for a reminder that, if the growth in abortion is to be checked and its effects to be minimized, the need is as great as ever for such organizations as LIFE and the Society for the Protection of Unborn Children.

1. *God Alive* (London, Darton Longman and Todd, 1981), p.28.
2. ibid., p.41.
3. *Tablet*, 2 July 1983, p.628.

Issues

1

Medical Aspects of Abortion

PHILIP R. NORRIS

Introduction

The Hippocratic Oath was formulated three hundred years
before the Christian era began. Over the centuries it became the
cornerstone of medical ethical practice throughout the civilized
world. On it was built the high reputation that doctors have
enjoyed ever since.

From a clinical point of view, the Oath contained two
fundamental principles. First, the doctor would prescribe only
for the good of his patient:

> I will follow that system of regimen which, according to my
> ability and judgement, I consider to be for the benefit of my
> patient.

Second, the doctor would not use his special position and skills
to kill, presumably even when offered bribes to do so:

> I will give no poison to anyone if asked nor suggest any such
> counsel.

Having established these principles, it is even more surprising that pagan physicians living in an age when human life was cheap, considered that the unborn baby was also entitled to their protection:

> ... and in like manner I will not give a woman a pessary to procure an abortion.

In 1948 the World Medical Association redrafted this Oath in modern terms, reaffirming that the doctor would "maintain the utmost respect for human life from the moment of its conception even under threat".

However, since the passing of the Abortion Act of 1967, more than two million unborn babies have been deliberately destroyed by doctors in England and Wales.

This surely must be one of the most blatant examples of the abandonment overnight of a time-honoured ethical principle by any professional body. It is even more disturbing when one considers that only twenty years before, doctors had specifically reaffirmed in Geneva their solemn dedication to preserve the sanctity of human life from the moment of its conception.

Why this has happened is complex, and it is not my purpose here to explore and analyze all the reasons. Only the medical aspect, probably the most important, will be detailed and discussed. Since the days of Hippocrates, the doctor, like the priest, has been privy to learning and knowledge not possessed by, nor at times shared with, the majority of the community. Their pronouncements, advice and actions have been accepted with trust and given an almost divine ordinance. "Subdivinity" is relatively harmless as long as there are built-in restrictions superimposed by a higher spiritual authority. Remove these restrictions and codes, and then humility vanishes, new gods appear, the methods of obtaining knowledge are unrestrained with the result that the application of this knowledge becomes multi-directional and subject to the whim of anyone capable of independent thought and action.

A public brought up in the belief that doctors are still motivated by the principles of the Hippocratic Oath, often support the pro-abortionists in a curiously naive way, since it is believed that no doctor would kill another human being. It follows, therefore, that since a doctor *does* kill a fetus it cannot be human, otherwise he would not have destroyed it.

In order to encourage and sustain this belief, and also possibly as a sop to his own conscience, the doctor has begun to employ medical jargon concerning the origins of human life, which, at best, contains some elements of truth. This essay is an attempt to put the record straight, because the ancient physician was frequently much nearer the truth than his modern counterpart. Research into human reproduction has become ever more complicated in its biological, physiological and genetic implications, and this has tempted the physician into the proverbial position of studying the trees while losing sight of the wood. In the context of the abortion issue, this means losing the awareness of human life and its inherent sanctity, which was emphasized with true clarity in the Hippocratic Oath.

1. The Beginning of Life

The human population of the earth at present is about four and a half billion, and for every one of these human beings, without exception, life began the moment an egg from the mother was fertilized by a sperm from the father. The unfertilized egg, or ovum, if left alone, perishes. Therefore, it cannot, by itself, be considered the start of a human being.

The sperm likewise disintegrates if not allowed to combine with its female counterpart, the ovum or egg. Therefore, no spermatazoon alone can be regarded as the start of a human being.

The gametes are not "human beings" by themselves. A human being must have started at fertilization and at no other point in time. There are some 4½ billion people on earth to prove it.

2. Sexual Intercourse

Except in a very few instances, fertilization is effected by an act of intercourse. It is recorded that some primitive peoples do not relate the act of sexual intercourse with the subsequent birth of a baby. Unhappily, in the past, we left our adolescents in the same state of ignorance. This error is now acknowledged by all enlightened communities; surely all adolescents, without exception, should be made aware that the purpose of depositing sperm into the female vagina is to facilitate fertilization and the creation of a new human being. This is a physiological truth that cannot be challenged. If a couple wish to enjoy the pleasure of sexual intercourse without the responsibility of procreation, that is another matter; but to try to change the truth and pretend that the sexual act was not designed for procreation is to degrade human intelligence.

3. Human Intra-uterine Life (Life before Birth)

To better understand human life before birth, we should consider the three successive phases of development, the *zygote* phase, the *embryonic* phase and the *fetal* phase.

(a) *The Zygote (morula) Phase of Human Development*   Fertilization, we believe, normally takes place at the end of the fallopian tube, and the fertilized egg (now called a zygote) moves down the tube towards the cavity of the uterus where it embeds in the uterine wall. The journey takes from four to seven days and during this time the single-celled zygote divides and subdivides until it resembles a microscopic mulberry; indeed it is often referred to as a "morula", Latin for a mulberry.

Our knowledge of this stage of development is very primitive. The cells appear to be identical in the very early stages of division and behave as though they were totipotent: that is to say, each cell, if separated from the bunch, could continue to develop as an independent zygote (morula), and if allowed to implant in the uterine wall, would eventually produce a human being identical to the one resulting from the original parent zygote. This is the process by which identical twins are created. (Dissimilar twins develop from two separate fertilized eggs). Later on, however, this totipotency is lost and the cells become more specialized, separating into two groups—one group forming the embryo (the human being proper)—the second group developing into the embryo's supporting tissue (the placenta and its membranes).

Other characteristics can be noted at this stage. Each cell in the zygote has a nucleus, and within the nucleus are 46 chromosomes. Half the chromosomes come from the mother and half come from the father through his sperm. It is on these chromosomes that the hereditary factors or genes are located. The arrangement and character of the genes is unique to each individual, and will never be possessed by any other human being in the history of mankind. The genes constitute an identikit picture of the "human-being to be". It is not unreasonable to predict that one day we will be able to recognize and forecast at a very early stage, the basic unmodified characteristics of that new human being by analysis of the chromosomes taken from a single nucleus (either embryonic or extra-embryonic).

(b) *The Embryonic Phase of Human Development*   This is the phase of anatomical development. Once the two main cell masses have been clearly differentiated,—the supportive cell mass (placenta and membranes), and the embryonic cell mass—the cells destined to become the new human being arrange themselves into systems: the skeletal system, the cardiovascular system, the nervous systems, the genito-urinary (kidney) system, the gastro-intestinal system, the endocrine system, and all those other parts that go to make up a human being.

During this stage, the zygote (morula) is renamed and called an *embryo*. Approximately four to six weeks after fertilization the new individual is anatomically complete; the parts are all there ready to be developed into functioning units. The baby has now reached the fetal period of development and is called a *fetus*.

(c) *The Fetal Phase of Human Development*   Just as the embryonic phase of human development may be called the phase of *anatomical* development, so the fetal phase may be described as the phase of *physiological* development, or maturation. This is designed to prepare the new human being for survival in air, and is the longest stage in a baby's intra-uterine development. The zygote (morula) phase lasts only from two to four weeks; the embryonic phase from four to six weeks, but the fetal phase requires many months, and at the end of this period the baby is ready to be born into an atmospheric environment.

It is very important to appreciate that all systems are not completed in unison, and the rates of growth are infinitely variable and inter-linked. As the new baby grows and becomes more complex, the maternal supply lines become stretched and overloaded, and to overcome this, a large supply depot, the placenta, is created. Materials from the mother are brought to the placenta and from this point onwards the fetus itself is responsible for their collection and re-distribution through its own blood system. Therefore it is not surprising that the fetal cardiovascular system is well advanced in the development of the new baby, and the heart can be seen contributing even in the embryonic phase.

The urinary system likewise functions early, and is working perfectly, long before birth. The skeleton and skin developments are more leisurely, and some parts are not complete even at birth. The skull, for example, with good reason, does not reach final completion and stability until well after birth.

Natural physiological retardation of function during intra-uterine life is well illustrated in the physiological development of the lungs. Clearly, the lungs are not required until birth is imminent. It is not to the advantage of the fetus to breathe in utero, although fetal chest movements can be seen. The alveoli (air sacs) of the lungs are therefore closed during fetal immersion in amniotic fluid, and the change to enable the lungs to expand and accept air begins only a few weeks before birth. This is one of the great problems facing the neonatal paediatrician when a baby is born prematurely. How can the lungs be made to function before they are ready to do so in the normal course of their development? What is the secret which would advance maturity of the lungs?

A word must also be said about the nervous system. Of all the great systems of the body, the nervous system must surely be the most complex, the most hard-working, the most sensitive, and the most easily damaged. Deprive the brain of oxygen for more than four minutes and it is permanently damaged. The co-ordinated well-being of the whole human body depends upon the integrity of the nervous system.

One might compare the nervous system with an electronic communication and functional system in which the connecting and coordinating links are laid down in a pattern but not necessarily simultaneously. Even at birth, only primitive basic nervous functions are present, and the miraculous development and expansion in the child's nervous system occurs only after birth. The movements of the hands, arms and legs become purposeful. The brain receives impulses from touch, sight, hearing and smell, and computes and integrates them so that the baby begins to understand, to learn, and initiate thought processes which are translated into action and desire. It is the nervous system which demonstrates most clearly the fact that development and eventual completeness cannot be pinpointed during either intra-uterine or extra-uterine growth.

One system, the immune system, is almost non-existent at birth. Protection is provided by the mother while the baby is in utero, although even here the protection does not exist if the mother herself is vulnerable. For example, in the case of German measles, infection in the mother crosses the placenta and the virus damages the developing embryo, resulting in physical and sometimes mental handicaps.

Breast feeding continues maternal protection, and in about six months after birth the baby's own defences are now biochemically programmed to give wider and increasing security from harmful agents which may penetrate its immediate defences.

Shakespeare's "seven ages" of "extra-uterine man" now begin, having been preceded by the three stages of "intra-uterine man". None of these stages degrades the preceding one as far as the humanity of the individual is concerned.

Medical Concepts employed to support Abortion

Fertilization, Conception and Implantation

There was a time when fertilization, conception and implantation were terms used to imply the same thing. This was understandable because in the past a woman did not know she was pregnant until she missed a menstrual period, by which time the zygote (fertilized egg) had implanted itself in the uterine wall—a sure sign, in the majority of cases, that the baby had successfully survived its tubal journey, probably the most hazardous period of its whole life.

It is essential that the whole truth about the commencement of human development is clarified. Conception is not synonymous with implantation. A new human being is conceived when the egg is fertilized by the sperm. This scientific truth must be allowed the utmost emphasis. We must discriminate between the terms fertilization and conception on the one hand, and the term implantation on the other. It is fertilization which conceives a new human life. Implantation occurs from four to seven days later and is merely one stage in the development of a mature human baby. Scientific accuracy and precision surely demand clarity of language, especially when dealing with the beginning of all human life?

The Beginning of Human Life

Human life begins at fertilization, despite numerous pseudo-medical claims to the contrary. It cannot be repeated too often that "time" provides the most convincing proof. Nine months after fertilization a child is born. This child is unique in itself, and will remain so, never to be duplicated throughout time.

It does not matter at what stage you kill "child unique", be it immediately after fertilization, before viability has been achieved in the womb, just before birth or after birth. At whatever stage the deed is done, "child unique" is killed. Everyone living today was once a zygote, an embryo and a fetus. A vacuum pump would have destroyed them just as effectively as a bullet, a car accident or a virulent virus. The earlier and more privately and speedily the deed is done, the more acceptable the act of abortion is perceived to be. Relief from an awkward situation readily facilitates the replacement of truth by contrived and plausible argument, coupled with the fact that the actual destruction of the baby often takes place while the mother is anaesthetized, and therefore detached from the process of killing (the father more often than not is ignored).

Wastage of Gametes

To use the argument in support of abortion that natural wastage of sperm and ova already occurs, is to employ a false parallel, because no sperm or egg containing a haploid (unpaired) complement of chromosomes can exist or develop as an individual. Of course, embryologists might artificially remedy this deficiency, but it does not alter the validity of the statements that have already been made.

"Out of sight, out of mind" once upon a time led to an understandable devaluation of the human fetus. Its presence as a living thing could easily be forgotten and the awareness conveniently used to create the myth that nothing important happened during an abortion. Ultrasound now gives a pictorial demonstration of the fetus as a living being. Yet even this vivid picture can be ignored, forgotten, or suppressed to justify an abortion. Once truth is aborted, society is threatened with dire consequences.

Natural Zygote (morula) and Fetal Wastage

We do not know precisely how many fertilized ova, embryos or fetuses are lost "naturally". The mere fact that sometimes things go wrong after fertilization, preventing further development and eventually killing the concepsus before it is born, is no more an excuse for destroying a normally developing baby than is the excuse that because "nature" kills thousands of born children and adults through disease, we therefore have a mandate to kill normal children and adults.

The Handicapped

Accidents occur before birth as they do after birth. The paraplegic as a result of spinabifida is no more or less handicapped from a physical point of view than thousands of other men and women who have sustained similar injuries after birth. Why then should the unborn be deprived of life because of his handicap, while his fellow human beings, who are similarly afflicted after birth, are allowed to live?

In fact, the unborn baby is, in some ways, more fortunate than his born counterpart. Firstly, the degree of handicap cannot be estimated accurately until after birth. Frequently this is less than originally feared and can be treated. Secondly, the shock of handicap is often harder to bear in a person who in the past has enjoyed good health with unrestricted freedom, than in one who has never known what it is to possess his or her full faculties. But do these factors weigh in favour of the unborn, and is the baby given the benefit of the doubt? In medical experience the usual answer is "No". Consider, for example, the tests for spina bifida. A raised alpha-fetoprotein level in the amniotic fluid often became a baby's death-warrant, even though it was known that the test is not 100 per cent accurate. Furthermore, the degree of handicap is not always related to the amount of alpha-fetoprotein detected. Fortunately, more accurate screening with ultrasound has now brought some precision into the investigation, and doctors are becoming more discriminating. Specimens taken from the patient can be used for diagnostic purposes to follow the course of treatment and to record its progress. Likewise, fluid and specimens taken from the concepsus (blood, urine, amniotic fluid) and from tissue biopsy can be taken from the unborn and used for the same purpose.

Obviously the techniques employed now are crude and not without risk to the fetus and the mother, but in the near future, the neonatal paediatrician and surgeon will be an essential member of an obstetric team. The emphasis at the moment is on genetic analysis and sex determination. Both are diagnostic at present, but no doubt treatment based on the genetic findings will eventually be available, and then the procedure will be therapeutic. However, until this occurs, the problems detected are far too frequently resolved by killing the unborn child. A doctor's refusal to determine the sex of an unborn baby for the sole purpose of destroying the unwanted sex—boy or girl—is sometimes greeted with surprise by the patient and can one wonder at this, when perfectly normal unborn babies, of either sex, are eliminated quite readily for reasons which, in many cases, are largely imaginary?

Dangers of Abortion and Associated Procedures

These are extensive—a short sample list follows:

Immediate
1. Bleeding (haemorrhage—could be fatal)
2. Collapse—anaesthetic, vaso-vagal
3. Tissue damage (perforated uterus, cervical tears)
4. Septicaemia—kidney failure

Later
1. Heavy periods (menorrhagia)
2. Severe monthly period pains (dysmenorrhea)
3. Acute/chronic infection:
   pelvic pain
   painful intercourse (dyspareunia)
   infertility
4. Miscarriages
5. Premature labour (usually incompetent cervix)
6. Psychological (often depression in later life)

The dangers inherent in all abortion procedures should not be used in the argument against abortion, because such dangers are being reduced daily, and once they have been removed by new techniques and skills, there will be nothing to argue about, and this form of opposition, like the house built on sand, will collapse.

However, this is not to say that the dangers should be ignored, but simply that they should not be used as the principle reason for refusing abortion. Some women contemplating an abortion may consider the dangers of the abortion more acceptable than carrying the baby to term, no matter how uncomplicated the pregnancy and subsequent confinement at term is likely to be. The plain truth is that they do not want the baby.

A normal pregnancy is intended to be protected by the mother against all assaults. There is nothing more stubborn than a well established pregnancy, as the old abortionists knew only too well. Today, however, with the powerful weapons of drugs and surgery, the walls of the citadel protecting the developing baby can be breached and the hapless living human being expelled from the uterus in spite of all the mother's physiological and anatomical efforts to retain it.

Damage is inevitable. Sometimes it is permanent and the uterus may never again recover. Sometimes it is limited and will be repaired in due course of time with or without the help of the medical profession, as in the case of a torn neck of the womb (cervix). This particular injury often manifests itself in repeated premature births or miscarriages before the damage is discovered.

During the abortion procedure, other destructive agents may gain access to the torn tissues and destroy the ability of the uterus to function again; the commonest example of this is blocked tubes by infection. There is also the consequence of heavy blood loss which may result in cerebral damage to the mother, or even death.

Finally, it is essential to be ever mindful that nothing can put the clock back; no matter how pressing the circumstances, the woman herself was responsible for the final decision to kill her baby. Often the psychological backlash is postponed until later in life, when, in the fading twilight, truth is acknowledged—sadly too late to redeem the life of the baby that should have been.

Misuse of Medical Terms to degrade the Unborn

The stages of development of the various systems that make up a human being have time-tables of their own which overlap and are coordinated according to their physiological requirement at the time of development. Once launched into the atmospheric environment, the systems are put to test, adjusted, and some continue development until finally completed.

To choose a moment during gestation and say this is human and this is not, is to profess ignorance of the anatomical and physiological development of the fetus. By attempting to use a moment of development as the criterion for deciding one baby should live and another not we establish a principle which could be employed after birth. To use such terms as zygote, embryo, fetus in order to suggest an inferior status to the human being is no more valid than to suggest that extra-uterine stages of development similarly grade a human being in importance. For example, is the toothless wonder, feeding at the breast, less valuable than the one now on solid food? Is the screaming crawler less valuable than the toddler? Are the members of a Primary School less valuable than those in the higher grades of education? And, what is more sinister, do we accept that the handicapped person—mentally or physically—is less valuable than his brighter or more perfectly formed brother or sister?

Notions such as these gain acceptance in theory and practice only too easily unless they are forcefully rejected at the outset.

Another argument used to degrade the fetus stresses certain parasitic-like features of its development. Superficially, the baby in utero could be described as a parasite in that he or she receives all from the mother and seemingly contributes nothing to her welfare. The status is not symbiotic (mutually beneficial). The mother can exist without the embryo or fetus; the developing human baby at this stage cannot continue life without its mother, or substitute mother. Closer examination of the situation reveals that this is not a true parasitic relationship, for the obvious reason that the host has actually created the "parasite". The true parasite is a completely separate organism living off another organism, be it the same species or not. There is more than a suspicion that those who use the word "parasite" in connection with the intra-uterine development of a human being are doing so not simply to describe its relationship to its parent, but in the hope that the unhealthy nature of some of the parasitic relationships will rub off on to the fetus and provide an excuse for destroying it.

Do we consider the old and infirm are parasites? Presumably they were not parasitic in the prime of their lives. Their contribution to the host (the community) was paid in advance. Likewise, the child is a temporary "parasite" in the basic material sense, and yet, even in the unborn state, the child is capable of contributing to the well being of the mother. One has only to witness the joy and happiness in any antenatal clinic.

Confusion over the Use of the Word "Viability"

There is no fixed age at which viability is achieved and no legal definition of viability. The Infant Life (Preservation) Act, 1929, speaks of a child "capable of being born alive". The World Health Organisation defines a live birth as follows: "Live birth is the complete expulsion or extraction from its mother of a product of conception irrespective of the duration of the pregnancy, which after such separation breathes or shows any other evidence of life, such as the beating of the heart, pulsation of the umbilical cord or definite movement of voluntary muscle whether or not the umbilical cord has been cut or the placenta is attached. Each product of such a birth is considered live born."

The mischief occurred when the Infant Life (Preservation) Act pronounced the gestational age of twenty-eight weeks or more as *prima facie* proof that a woman was pregnant "of a child capable of being born alive". This figure of twenty-eight weeks has long ceased to have any medical credibility. The age of survival is dropping year by year, and there will come a time when the smallest zygote will be capable of being nurtured until it has reached the stage of viability.

The abortionists have made use of this arbitrary figure in order to justify the baby's destruction. The truth of the matter is that viability can be demonstrated with accuracy only after the child has been born and given all possible medical assistance. But no abortionist wants to assist the unborn baby. He has contracted to destroy it.

Termination and Abortion

These two terms are often confused. Every pregnancy at some stage has to be terminated, and there is no doubt that there are conditions which develop during a pregnancy making the conti- nuance of the pregnancy hazardous. In such cases, treatment of the mother is, medically, treatment indirectly of the baby. If treatment of the mother is failing, or if the treatment requires the use of drugs which cross the placental barrier to harm the baby, then clearly the baby must be removed from the uterus if it is to have any chance of survival. Herein lies the difference between a therapeutic termination of pregnancy and an abortion. The terms are not synonymous. The Shorter Oxford English Dictionary defines abortion as "the procuring of premature delivery so as to destroy the offspring". A true therapeutic termination of pregnancy has every facility available at the time of the baby's birth, to save it, as well as its mother. If, on the other hand, it is the intention of the physician to destroy the baby, then this can only be an abortion. (The 1967 Abortion Act uses the phrase "termination of pregnancy" to describe an abortion. This distortion of language has confused some people.)

Epilogue

When all is said and done, there is nothing new that the sciences of physiology, embryology and medicine have dis- covered to alter the truth about the unborn child's humanity.

Doctors, like other members of society, do not find it easy to swim against the tide of popular opinion. Lip service is paid to the Hippocratic Oath, and the majority of modern doctors have probably read it only superficially and have not personally solemnized it as an Oath, which they intend to observe faithfully throughout their professional lives. Certainly it is not an Oath universally taken at graduation and, where it is formally recited, the majority of newly qualified doctors forget it as soon as the last sentence has been uttered. At the same time the general public still assume that their doctors subscribe to the traditional Oath and ethical code. One Greek doctor, when asked if he knew who Hippocrates was, expressed astonishment at such a question being put to a "descendant" of the Great Physician. Did he take the Hippocratic Oath? "Why yes, of course." Did he do abortions? "Yes, I do." But when asked how he reconciled the two, he merely grinned, shrugged his shoulders and vanished. At least he was better than the British Professor of Obstetrics who, when confronted with the World Medical Association's modern version of the Hippocratic Oath, did not know it, or even how it had originated. The Oath is now a mere theatrical expression and has been conveniently forgotten by the modern physician.

APPENDIX

1. *The Hippocratic Oath*

I swear by Apollo the physician and Aesculapius and Health and All-Heal, and all the gods and goddesses, that, according to my ability and judgment I will keep this Oath and this stipulation—to reckon him who taught me this Art equally dear to me as my parents, to share my substance with him and relieve his necessities if required; to look upon his off-spring as equal to my own brothers, and to teach them this Art if they shall wish to learn it, without fee or stipulation; and that by precept, lecture, and every mode of instruction I will impart a knowledge of the Art to my own sons and those of my teachers, and to disciples bound by a stipulation and an oath of obedience to the law of medicine, but to none other.

I will follow that system of regimen, which, according to my ability and judgment, I consider to be for the benefit of my patients, and abstain from whatever is deleterious and mischievous. I will give no poison to anyone if asked, nor suggest any such counsel; and in like manner I will not give to a woman a pessary to produce abortion. With purity and with holiness I will pass my life and practise my Art. I will not cut persons suffering from stone but will leave that to be done by men who are practitioners of this work.

Into whatever houses I enter I will go into them for the benefit of the sick, and will abstain from all intentional mischief and harm, especially from the seduction of females or males, freemen or slaves. Whatever, in connection with my professional practice, or even outside of it, I see or hear in the life of men, which ought not to be spoken of abroad, I will not divulge, reckoning that all such things should be kept secret.

While I continue to keep this Oath unviolated may it be granted to me to enjoy life and the practice of the Art among men for all time! But should I trespass and violate this Oath may the reverse be my lot!

2. *Declaration of Geneva (1948)*

At the time of being admitted as a Member of the medical profession I solemnly pledge myself to consecrate my life to the service of humanity;

I will give to my teachers the respect and gratitude which is their due;

I will practise my profession with conscience and dignity;

The health and life of my patient will be my first consideration;

I will respect the secrets which are confided in me;

I will maintain by all the means in my power, the honour and the noble traditions of the medical profession;

My colleagues will be my brothers;

I will not permit considerations of religion, nationality, race, party politics or social standing to intervene between my duty and my patient;

I will maintain the utmost respect for human life, from the time of its conception, even under threat, I will not use my medical knowledge contrary to the laws of humanity;

I make these promises solemnly, freely and upon my honour ... *The Second General Assembly of the World Medical Association, 1948.*

2

Personhood and the Ethics of Abortion

J. FOSTER

I

Let me begin by saying what I mean by 'abortion'. As a medical term, the word 'abortion' is often used as a synonym for 'miscarriage'. In this medical sense, we may speak of an abortion even when the miscarriage is purely accidental, e.g. the result of a fall. But outside the medical world, the term 'abortion' is normally reserved for cases in which the miscarriage is deliberately induced—cases in which someone deliberately terminates the pregnancy with the intention of destroying the fetus. It is this sort of abortion—the deliberate destruction of the fetus—with which I shall be primarily concerned and which, in what follows, I shall use the word 'abortion' to signify. It should be noted that abortion in this sense is to be distinguished, not only from cases of accidental miscarriage, but also from cases in which, when the pregnancy is deliberately terminated, the death of the fetus is foreseen, but not intended. This does not mean that my discussion of abortion will have no bearing on these cases. But it does mean that the evaluation of these cases will not be my primary concern.

There is one further point of terminology. Strictly speaking, the term 'fetus' applies to the prenatal organism only after it has reached a certain stage of development. Prior to that stage, it is called an 'embryo' or, immediately after fertilization, a 'zygote'. But while I shall continue to use these latter terms in their proper (restricted) sense, I shall use the term 'fetus' in a broader sense, to signify the prenatal organism at any stage of development— any stage from conception (i.e. fertilization) to birth. This will be convenient and will not, I think, lead to any lack of clarity.

I hold that abortion, as defined, is morally wrong. I also hold that it is the sort of moral offence which should be legally prohibited. The purpose of this paper is to provide a detailed defence of these views. But I shall start by putting my case in its simplest terms:

> The fetus is a human being (and is so in the fullest sense). Except (perhaps) as a judicial execution (and then only of someone whose crime merits the death-penalty) or, in certain extreme cases, as a defensive measure against an aggressor, the deliberate killing of another human being is a grave violation of natural justice. Such killing is, to put it bluntly, murder. Thus abortion, the deliberate killing of the human fetus, is morally wrong, and to be legally prohibited, because it is a form of murder.

Some people may think that, even from the standpoint of the anti-abortionist, my use of the term 'murder' here is inappropriate, both because, in certain circumstances, abortion is legally permissible and because, even when illegal, it is not, for legal purposes, classified as murder. If anyone wants to restrict the term 'murder' to its legal sense, I have no objection; I am happy to re-express the claim that abortion is murder as the claim that it is, morally speaking, tantamount to murder. The important point is that, as I see it, there is no morally relevant difference between deliberately killing a human being who has been born and deliberately killing a human being who is still inside his mother. If there is a legal difference, so much the worse for the law.

I have claimed that abortion is, or is morally tantamount to, murder. My defence of this claim will turn on two central issues, one concerning the status of the fetus (Is the fetus really a human being and is it so in every morally relevant sense?), the other concerning the ethics of abortion (Are there circumstances in which abortion is morally permissible or, at least, not tantamount to murder?). My discussion of the second issue will, of course, be strongly conditioned by my discussion of the first. For our moral evaluation of abortion obviously depends, to a considerable extent, on what sort of an entity we take the fetus to be, or perhaps (to allow for a view which I shall mention later) what sort of an entity we take the fetus to embody.

II

I have said that the fetus is a human being. And by this I mean that it is a human being right from conception, right from the time when the mother's egg is fertilized, when the egg and the sperm combine to form a single cell. But is this really so? If you look at a fertilized egg under a microscope, you do not see something which looks much like a human being, as we ordinarily think of one. There is no head or body, no arms or legs, and there are no internal organs. It is true that all these things develop very quickly. After a few weeks there is no mistaking the distinctively human form and organization. But at conception itself there is just one cell. How could anyone suppose this to be a genuine human being? To do so seems, on the face of it, to be as crazy as thinking that you have built a house as soon as you have laid the first brick. This is an important challenge to my position. For if there is an initial phase of development during which the fetus does not qualify as a human being, then there is an initial phase during which abortion would not count as murder.

Opponents of abortion sometimes try to meet this challenge by posing one of their own. If human life does not begin at conception, when does it begin? At what point in its development, whether prenatal or postnatal, does the organism become a genuine human being? Because the development is so gradual, any answer seems quite arbitrary. Apart from conception, there is no momentary change sufficiently decisive to constitute a definite transition of the organism from its pre-human to its human state. However, this point is not as telling as it seems. When a house is being constructed, we cannot, without arbitrariness, identify the moment when the house comes into existence. There is no critical episode of brick-laying which constitutes the definite transition from a building which is not a house to one that is. But we can be quite sure that the house did not come into existence at the moment when the first brick was laid. Likewise, it may be argued, we can be quite sure that human life does not begin at conception (or any earlier), even though its subsequent beginning cannot, without arbitrariness, be precisely dated.

To meet this argument, I need some positive reason for taking conception as the decisive point. Such a reason emerges when we examine the supposed analogy between fetal development and house-building more closely. For on closer inspection, what stand out are not the similarities but the differences between the two cases. Here are three crucial differences:

(1) The first brick to be laid does not contain a plan of what the completed house will be like. But the fertilized egg (the zygote) does contain a plan of what the completed adult will be like. It contains this plan in its genes. Almost every anatomical feature of the adult-to-be (both the features which make him distinctively human and the features which distinguish him from other people) is specified in the genetic blueprint which is formed, inside the zygote, at conception. Thus, unlike the brick, the zygote contains, as it were, the architect's drawings and instructions.

(2) After laying the first brick, the builder cannot just leave it to grow into a house. The brick will not grow into a house even if the builder inscribes the architect's plans on its surface and leaves a pile of bricks and mortar within easy reach. The brick will not grow, because it is not a living organism. But the zygote is a living organism and it will grow into something which is recognizably human just by drawing nourishment from its mother's body. In this sense, the zygote not only contains the architect's drawings, but also possesses the skills of the builder as well. It contains a plan of its subsequent development and the capacity to execute this plan on the raw materials at hand.

(3) To build a house, we have to keep on adding new bricks to those that are already in place. Once laid, each brick remains unchanged as the rest of the house is constructed. But the human fetus develops by a process of cell division. The fertilized egg grows and divides, each of these new cells grows and divides, and so on until (and after) the

adult form is reached. What we have here is a single expanding organism, rather than lots of separate bits and pieces which someone sticks together.

These three points may not settle the whole issue. But, collectively, they do establish something of crucial importance. They establish that, considered in purely biological terms, the human being comes into existence at conception. All subsequent development is just the process by which the human organism which already exists gradually realizes its inherent potential. The prenatal development and the postnatal development are just different phases in the history of a single biological entity. In biological terms, there is no more reason to deny the humanity of the zygote, when compared with the new-born baby, than to deny the humanity of the new-born baby, when compared with the schoolchild. This much at least is beyond dispute, once the biological facts are known.

It may be argued, however, that what really matters, for the issue of abortion, is not when the human organism begins, but when it becomes, as we may say, a *person*—when it becomes some*one* rather than just some*thing*. The abortionist must concede that a fetus is, in biological terms, a human being; but he may still deny that it is a person, or deny that it is a person right from conception. And if a fetus is not a person, then it is not even a human being in the morally relevant sense—the sense required to sustain my charge that abortion is tantamount to murder. For obviously, abortion can only be tantamount to murder if there is someone (a person) whom it kills. It would not be tantamount to murder if its only effect was to prevent a biological organism from developing to the point at which the person comes into existence. Of course, it would not follow from this that the destruction of the pre-personal fetus was morally permissible. But it would mean that any case against abortion would have to be formulated in a different way. And it would also mean, I think, that if the abortion of a pre-personal fetus is a moral offence, it is not an offence of the gravity I have supposed.

Why should anyone think that the fetus is not a person or not a person right from conception? The usual argument is that, in the very earliest phase of its existence, before it has developed a working brain, the fetus has no mind. It cannot think or feel or perceive. It lacks the capacity for conscious experience. The word 'capacity' needs to be emphasized here. Obviously, someone who is asleep may be wholly unconscious. But he still retains the capacity for consciousness, even if it is one which he cannot exercise in his present circumstances. The neural structures required for consciousness are intact, even if their functioning is temporarily suppressed. The point about the primitive fetus is that it lacks the capacity for consciousness altogether. The neural structures required for consciousness have yet to be formed. The brain has yet to develop, or has yet to achieve sufficient complexity to allow thought or experience to occur. This, it may be claimed, establishes that there is room for an early abortion in which no *person* is destroyed. It may be impossible to determine just how complex the brain must become before the capacity for consciousness is achieved. But at least, it will be said, we can be sure that the fetus is not a person in the first week or so after conception, before it has a nervous system at all. And while this may have little relevance to abortion as traditionally practised, it is of crucial relevance in evaluating something like the post-coital pill.

At first sight this argument seems quite plausible; but its plausibility evaporates when we become aware of its implications. One of its implications is that a new-born baby is not a genuine person—at least not in a sense which would give it a higher moral standing than, for example, an adult cat or a chimpanzee. For while a new-born baby certainly has a capacity for consciousness, it is clearly not in virtue of that capacity, or any of its *actual* mental capacities at that stage of its life, that we count it as a person in the morally relevant sense. Otherwise, we should have to count adult cats and chimpanzees as persons too, or at least as enjoying the same moral status, since their mental capacities are not inferior to those of a baby. Indeed, the adult chimpanzee's capacities are presumably superior. So if we want to accord babies a higher moral standing than cats and chimpanzees, as we presumably do, and if we think that this superior moral standing is in some way a consequence of superior mental capacities, or, perhaps better, of superior mental and spiritual capacities, then we shall have to say that it is the baby's *potential*, not its *actual*, capacities which are crucial—that the baby qualifies as a person, in the morally relevant sense, in virtue of its *potential* to develop, mentally and/or spiritually, in a certain way. But this will commit us to regarding the fetus as a person right from conception. For since the fertilized egg has the potential to develop into the new-born baby, it has the potential to acquire whatever characteristics the baby has the potential to acquire.

The importance of potential can be brought out in another way. Suppose someone, a normal intelligent adult, is involved in a road accident which destroys a portion of his brain. The portion thus destroyed is, we will suppose, one which is required for consciousness—one without which the patient is unable to think, feel or perceive. In all other respects, we will suppose, the patient's body continues to function in the normal way; in particular, the actions of the heart, lungs, kidneys and intestines are unaffected. Since he has lost his capacity for consciousness (or, as we may say, lost his mind), we may wonder whether the patient is, as a person, really alive. And the question may have some practical importance. Should we continue to feed and nurse him? Should we give him antibiotics when he gets an infection? Could we legitimately remove his kidneys and transplant them to someone else who needs them? There is room for controversy here. But one thing is clear. Suppose we know that over the next few months, if we continue to feed him, new brain cells will develop to replace the ones destroyed, so that he will eventually regain his capacity for consciousness and be able to function as a normal person. Knowing this, we would not regard him as currently dead for any practical purposes. We would say that to remove his kidneys now, and so (by terminating his life as a biological organism) prevent the regeneration of his brain and the restoration of consciousness, was nothing short of murder. We would say that, for all practical purposes, he is still, as a person, alive, simply because his capacity for consciousness will return, if we let it. Now I know that, as things are, brains do not regenerate. Once a part of the brain has been destroyed, then, short of a miracle, it is lost for ever. So the case I have just described is, as we say, only hypothetical. But it helps us to see more clearly the true situation of the fetus in its precerebral state. For there is no doubt in this case that, if it continues to draw nourishment from its mother, the fetus will develop a brain and acquire the capacity for consciousness. And surely this means that, for all practical purposes, the fetus qualifies as a person right from conception.

For if the potential to regain the capacity for consciousness is decisive in the case of the brain damaged adult, surely the potential to acquire this capacity must be equally decisive in the case of the precerebral fetus, granted that the fetus qualifies as a human being in all the biological respects.

It might be objected that the potential to regain a capacity is not the same as the potential to acquire one for the first time and that this difference should make a difference to the way we interpret the two cases. Thus it might be claimed that the potential to acquire the capacity for consciousness is sufficient for personhood only if the capacity is one which the human organism possessed at some earlier time. This would mean that, with such a potential, the brain-damaged adult would qualify as a person, but the precerebral fetus would not. However, I can see no rational basis for distinguishing the cases in this way. For, although we may feel a deeper commitment to those whom we have known as persons, the previous history of an organism cannot, as such, be relevant to determining its present status. Nor would we be tempted to regard it as relevant were it not for another factor which is liable to distort our judgment in these cases. Thus if it could be shown that it is only four weeks after birth (i.e. birth at full term) that the neural structures become sufficiently complex to sustain a capacity for consciousness, we would not, on that basis, deny that a baby of only 27 days counted as a person, in any sense relevant to determining its right to life. The real reason why we are tempted to downgrade the fetus is that, being concealed and, in its earliest stage, being of a less recognizably human form, it does not automatically elicit the sympathy and concern we feel for those who are more visibly members of our community.

We have been considering the question of whether the preconscious fetus qualifies as a person. But it might be argued that this very question is misconceived. It might be argued that a person is not, strictly speaking, a physical organism, but something purely spiritual. The real *me* is not this body, but something which, as it were, inhabits it and which may survive after my body has passed away. So perhaps what is really at issue is: at what point, in the history of the organism, does this spiritual entity (the soul) enter the body? Does it enter at conception, or when the brain is formed, or at quickening, or at birth, or still later? If it enters at some point after conception, then abortion prior to that point is not tantamount to murder. The destruction of the fetus does not count as the killing of a person (i.e. the separating of soul from body) since there is no embodied person to be killed.

It is far from clear that we should accept this 'Cartesian' conception of a person as a non-physical, purely spiritual entity. Certainly, most philosophers would not. But even if we do (and I myself find it attractive), I see no grounds for revising our conclusion about the point when personal life begins. We might concede, for the sake of argument, that until the fetus has a working brain, the soul and the body will not interact in the ordinary sense. The soul will not experience anything as a result of what is taking place in the body and it will not be able to act on the body in the way in which I can now move my limbs. But this does not mean that before it has a working brain, the fetus does not possess a soul. Given the biological significance of conception, it seems very likely that the soul comes into existence at the same time and that it is attached to the zygote in virtue of the fact that its potential to acquire a subsequent mental life is inextricably bound up with the zygote's potential to develop a brain. I admit that this conclusion is less than certain (or would be without the theological point that I shall mention in a moment), since, in the nature of things, the creation of the soul is not something which we can scientifically detect. But if there is room for doubt, we are morally obliged to give the zygote the benefit of it. If there is a reasonable chance that the zygote embodies a person, we should act on the presumption that it does, just as, if there is a reasonable chance that an accident victim is still alive, we should act on the presumption that he is. It would be far worse to fail to accord the zygote the respect to which it is entitled than to accord it a respect to which it is not.

There is still one final objection to be considered. If, as I am contending, the fetus is, or embodies, a person right from conception, how are we to interpret the case of monozygotic twins—the case where the zygote divides and the two halves develop as separate, though genetically identical, organisms? If we say that each twin has been a person from conception, we are forced to say either that a single person has become two persons or that, before the split, there are two persons with a single body.

And, at first sight, neither of these conclusions seems plausible. Consequently, it is sometimes concluded that each of the two persons comes into being at or after the time of the organic division and that, prior to that time, the undivided organism neither is nor embodies a person at all. But if we say this in the case of twins, it becomes difficult, even in the case of a normal pregnancy, to think of the person as beginning at conception. It becomes hard to avoid the conclusion that the organism becomes, or comes to embody, a person only when it has developed to a point at which twinning is no longer biologically possible. And such a conclusion would allow a very early abortion, of a pre-personal fetus, to escape from the kind of moral objection which I have raised.

This is an ingenious argument, but, nonetheless, wholly fallacious. For let us imagine a fictitious world in which twinning can occur not only in the earliest phase of pregnancy, but also much later, when it is uncontrovertible that the organism which divides already is, or embodies, a person. Let us imagine, for example, a world in which a child of five is capable of growing into a pair of, as it were, siamese twins, which then separate and live as distinct persons. As things are, of course, this is (and fortunately so) biologically impossible. But the thought-experiment is enough for my purposes. For clearly, in such an imaginary case, we do not want to say that, prior to the twinning, there is no person. But if so, then the phenomenon of zygotic twinning is simply irrelevant to the question of whether personal life begins at conception. This question has to be decided on other grounds, and I have already indicated why I think we should answer it in the affirmative.

There remains, of course, the intriguing question of whether, in the case of monozygotic twins, there are two persons or only one prior to the split. There are some deep philosophical issues here, which I shall not go into. Let me just say this: essentially, the answer we give will depend on whether we think of a person as a human organism with a mental and spiritual aspect or as an immaterial soul or spirit which inhabits a body. If we think in the first way, we will say that one person becomes two. If we think in the second way, we will say that two persons are attached to the original zygote. I could say much more about this, but I can see no point in doing so in the context of this paper. All that matters, for our present concern, is that personal life starts at conception, whatever sort of entity we take a person to be and however the lives of twin persons are related prior to their corporeal division.

In discussing the status of the human fetus, I have not, as yet, made any appeal to doctrines of a distinctively Christian kind. The claim that human and personal life begins at conception is one which I have defended solely on the basis of the biological findings and rational argument. However, it is worth noting, indeed stressing, that the claim is also one which, for independent reasons, Christians are obliged to accept. For it is entailed by the doctrine of the Incarnation as traditionally interpreted.

According to this doctrine, at a certain point in human history God the Son, the Second Person of the Trinity, became a man. In becoming a man he did not, of course, cease to be God. He retained his eternal divine nature, but in addition took human nature, and lived a normal human life with a normal human body and a normal human mind. All this is a very large and complicated theological subject, but I want us to focus on just one question. At what point in the development of the human organism did the Incarnation occur? Exactly when, in this developmental process, did the Son take human nature and begin his human life? The answer is implicit in the Gospel records of Matthew and Luke, whose accounts are distilled in the two credal claims: 'He was conceived by the Holy Spirit' and 'He was incarnate by the Holy Spirit of the Virgin Mary and was made man.' Clearly, the conception by the Spirit referred to in the Apostles' Creed is the same as the Incarnation by the Spirit referred to in the Nicene Creed. So conception is marked out as the moment of incarnation—the moment when God took human nature, when Christ began his human life. Now, of course, since Mary was a virgin, this conception did not involve fertilization in the ordinary biological sense. But obviously it must have occurred at the same point in the biological process as fertilization occurs in the ordinary case, and it must have resulted in a conceptus of the normal human type. This means that in the ordinary case conception (i.e. fertilization) must be the beginning of human life. For Christ could hardly have taken human nature at a point prior to that at which, in the ordinary case, human life begins. And, in particular, it means that, in the ordinary case, conception (i.e. fertilization) must be the beginning of personal life. For the Son could hardly have taken human nature at a point when, in the ordinary case, the human organism would not yet qualify as, or embody, a person.

This argument, of course, will cut no ice with non-Christians. And even Christians, or so-called Christians, might try to resist it in one of two ways. In the first place, someone might claim that, contrary to the creeds and Gospel records, the Incarnation took place at some point after conception, the conception itself being effected in the normal biological way by the fusion of an egg and a sperm. Secondly, someone who claims to be a Christian might deny the Incarnation altogether or give it some metaphorical interpretation (e.g. that God adopts Jesus as his proxy on earth). I do not have space here to discuss these positions in any detail. Briefly, my objection to the first is that it is incoherent. If the egg is fertilized in the normal biological way and possesses its person-hood or potential for personhood prior to any incarnational inter-vention by the Holy Spirit, then the Son has lost his opportunity to be the person in question. For the person's identity is already fixed by factors which are independent of the Incarnation (factors derived from the natural process of human reproduction), and the Son cannot become that person without ceasing to be him-self. My objection to the second position is simply that the Incarnation, in its literal sense, is absolutely essential and fundamental to the Christian Faith. Unless God has done some-thing for humanity *from the inside*, the Christian doctrine of salvation collapses; and without the doctrine of salvation, there is no Christian gospel at all.

III

Let us then take it as settled that, right from conception, a fetus is a human being in the fullest sense, by which I mean not only that it satisfies the biological criteria for being human (for being a member of the species *homo sapiens*), but also that it is (or embodies) a person—that it is some*one*, not just some*thing*. On this basis, I claim that abortion, the deliberate destruction of the fetus, is, or is morally tantamount to, murder. But not everyone who would accept my account of the status of the fetus would accept this moral conclusion. So our next task must be to look into the objections which they might raise.

If abortion is tantamount to murder, it is not only a grave moral offence; it is also a serious violation of natural justice. Consequently, my moral evaluation of abortion entails a two-fold obligation. In the first place, since abortion is morally wrong, we have a moral duty not to perform or procure it. Secondly, since it is a violation of natural justice, we have a moral duty to do all that is reasonable to prevent its occurrence. This means, in particular, that abortion is the sort of offence which should be legally prohibited. Its potential victims, like the potential victims of other forms of murder, are entitled to the protection of the criminal law. If abortion is tantamount to murder, we cannot regard it, as we might regard homosexual activity, as something which, while morally reprehensible, people should have the liberty to engage in if they wish.

It is at this point that the first objection to my position could be raised. For it might be argued that, in pressing the claims of the fetus, I am ignoring the rights of the mother. 'The mother' it will be claimed, 'has rights over the use of her own body. Her body is, in effect, her property, and although the baby is not part of her body, but a separate organism, she has the right to decide whether or not he should stay inside and draw nourishment from it. Just as a householder is at liberty to expel an uninvited visitor, so the mother should be at liberty to expel an unsolicited baby and enlist the help of others (i.e. the medical practitioners) to accomplish this. Of course, the mother should take account of the fact that the baby is, like herself, a human being in the fullest sense, and this may dissuade her from having an abortion, even if she regrets the baby's existence. But it is she who has the right to decide the issue—the right to weigh the life of the baby against her own interests and have an abortion if she chooses. We may criticize such a choice as selfish, unless there are extenuating circumstances, but we should not regard it as the sort of offence—a breach of natural justice—which it is the business of the law to prohibit. We should not insist that the mother put her body at the disposal of the baby, just as we should not insist that someone donate a portion of his blood to save the life of an accident victim.

As it stands, this argument is not very convincing. For there is scarcely any analogy between the householder's innocuous expulsion of an intruder and the abortionist's destruction of a human life. Of course, we can make the cases more analogous by supposing the expulsion to be violent. But unless the violence can be justified on grounds of self-defence (or defence of one's family), the only effect of this will be to turn the act of expulsion itself into a criminal offence. If I throw someone from a high window and he dies as a result of the injuries sustained, it is no defence against the charge of murder that the victim had no business to be in my house.

However, there is another analogy which might serve the purposes of the argument more effectively.[1] Suppose I wake one morning to find that someone else, whose kidneys have failed, has been attached to me in a way that allows my kidneys to function for both of us. Let us further suppose that (1) he was attached without my consent and without his knowledge or consent, (2) he is at present unconscious, but will regain consciousness, in due course, if he stays attached, (3) it will take about nine months to cure his kidney ailment, but if he is detached before the cure is complete, he will die almost immediately, and (4) his attachment, though very inconvenient to me, does not endanger my life or pose a serious threat to my health. The question is: ought I to be legally entitled to detach him if I choose? The answer, it seems clear, is that I ought. Such detachment would not, it seems, constitute a serious breach of natural justice which it should be the business of the law to prohibit. For the kidney patient is not entitled to the use of my body without my consent, even if he needs my body for his survival. But if so, then surely, it will be argued, the fetus is not entitled to the use of his mother's body without her consent. Admittedly, the question of consent is more complicated in this case. For we might deem the woman to have given her consent, at least in terms that are relevant to natural justice, if she consented to the sexual act by which the fetus was conceived. And if this is so, the fact that she wants the pregnancy to be terminated would not suffice to make the two cases analogous. But we can get over this by focusing on the special case in which the sexual act did not have the woman's consent. Surely, in this case at least, where the pregnancy is the

---

1. The example which follows is based on one devised by J.J. Thomson in 'A Defence of Abortion', *Philosophy & Public Affairs*, Vol. 1 No. 1, 1971.

result of rape, the woman has the right to detach the fetus whose existence has been forced on her, in the same way that I have the right to detach the kidney-patient whose attachment has been forced on me.

This brings us to a further and perhaps the most crucial point. As I have defined it, abortion is the deliberate destruction of the fetus—the termination of the pregnancy with the intention of killing the fetus. The case of the kidney-patient is simply irrelevant to abortion in this sense, since no one could suggest that the rights I have over my body entitle me to act with the intention of killing the person attached to me. If I were entitled to detach him with the intention of killing him, I would be equally entitled to choose some other method of killing him, e.g. by shooting or poisoning. And clearly I am not. Hence, the case of the kidney-patient does not even provide *prima facie* grounds for permitting abortion in the relevant sense. It might seem that this point cuts both ways. For those who are not too concerned about the preservation of fetal life might claim that it is at least permissible to *extract* the fetus (without direct assault) provided the sole aim of the operation is to ease the plight of the mother and provided the *death* of the fetus, while anticipated, is not seen as the means to that end. But nothing I have said provides any justification for such a claim. What I have said is that the intentional destruction of the fetus is tantamount to murder. It does not follow from this that every case in which the death of the fetus is foreseen, but not intended, is morally permissible nor even that it is not tantamount to murder. Rather, we should evaluate such cases on their merits. There is obviously, for example, a big difference between extracting the fetus as the only way of saving the mother's life and extracting it as the only way of keeping her slim enough to win a beauty competition. Given that the fetus is a human being in the fullest sense, the principle we must work with is that the fetus deserves the same respect and has the same *prima facie* right to protection as anyone else. There are, occasionally, situations where the lives of the mother and the fetus cannot both be preserved. In such situations, it is probably legitimate to preserve the mother's life at the expense of the fetus. But it is not legitimate to sacrifice the fetus in situations where both lives can be saved, even if the death of the fetus is only a foreseen, not an intended consequence.

It may be objected that I have dealt with the case of rape in an unduly cold and legalistic way.★ Thus it might be argued that what we have to consider, in such a case, are not merely the extent of the woman's rights over her own body and the extent of the fetus's rights to intra-uterine life, but also the woman's psychological state. Even if the pregnancy is not a continuation of the original assault, it is liable to prolong the trauma of that assault. From the woman's point of view the pregnancy may well be seen as adding insult to injury; she may well regard it as the tangible evidence of her humiliation—as a constant reminder to her and a public manifestation to others of the violation of her body. There is no denying that the continuation of the pregnancy is likely to involve, for the woman, a considerable amount of suffering—suffering which she in no way deserves and which an abortion would avoid. Moreover, once the baby is born she will be faced with the agonizing choice between rearing him herself and adoption. All this may suggest that, in such circumstances, the termination of the pregnancy would be the lesser of two evils —or, at least, that the woman should be allowed to decide the matter for herself. It is easy for an academic philosopher, in a cool moment of reflection, to say that abortion is wrong. But how can one, in all compassion, impose such a judgment on someone for whose suffering abortion may be the only remedy?

This is an ingenious argument. But, even in the case of the rape-induced pregnancy, it is not, I think, successful. The first point to notice is that the two situations are still not analogous in all morally relevant respects. One obvious difference is that the attachment of the fetus to the mother is in line with the natural functioning of both parties, while the attachment of the kidney-patient to me is not. The womb is biologically designed to house and nourish the fetus and the fetus is biologically designed to be housed and nourished in the womb. But my body is not designed to service the kidney-patient nor is his designed to be thus serviced by me. Given the biological facts, it is hard to think of the baby as trespassing on his mother's body, in the way we think of the kidney-patient as trespassing on mine. It is much easier to think of the baby as possessing a natural right to intra-uterine

★ For a different approach, see pp. 68-69.

life, not dependent on his mother's consent, just as he will possess a natural right to live outside his mother once he has been born. Moreover, and perhaps more importantly, while in both cases the situation is one which casually results from an act of injustice—an act which seriously violates a person's rights over his or her own body—in the case of the kidney patient, the situation is one which, in a sense, perpetuates this act, while, in the case of the fetus, it does not. For, in the one case, it is the act of attaching the patient to my body which constitutes the violation of my rights, while in the other case, it is the sexual act of the rapist, not the resulting conception and implantation, which constitutes the violation of the woman's rights. Consequently, there is a clear sense in which, by detaching the kidney-patient, I am merely defending myself against the continued violation of my rights; I am merely restoring the corporeal 'privacy' to which I am entitled and which the original act of attachment undermined. But in procuring an abortion, the woman is not defending herself against the continued violation of her rights. For it was the sexual assault which violated her rights, and the resulting pregnancy is not a continuation of that assault, even if it is something which she regrets. It has to be conceded, of course, that, since the kidney patient did not consent to his attachment and is unconscious at the time when I have to make my decision, neither the original act of injustice nor its perpetuation are things for which he is morally responsible. But his innocence cannot afford him any right to remain attached against my will. The most it can afford him is the right not to be *deliberately* harmed—a right which those responsible for the act of injustice have forfeited. But in detaching him, I am not deliberately harming him. I am merely deliberately protecting myself from a certain kind of harm, even though I foresee, without intending, his death as a consequence. (Incidentally, although the kidney-patient has no right to stay attached without my consent, I think that, other things being equal, I ought to give my consent.)

In answer to this, I would make three points. The first, and most important one, is that while it is certainly our duty to act with compassion towards the mother (as, indeed, towards all who suffer), the fact that an act is motivated by compassion does not guarantee that it is morally permissible. In particular, and this is just a truism, an act, however compassionate, is not morally permissible if it is a violation of the moral law. Thou shalt love thy neighbour as thyself, but not at the expense of killing someone else. The second point is that, in many cases, abortion will serve, in the long term, only to worsen the plight of the mother. For, while an abortion may help to relieve the trauma of rape, it is also likely to leave her with a burden of guilt—especially when she reflects on the fact that it is her own child whose destruction she has permitted. Moreover, this burden of guilt will be one which it is much harder to relieve than the earlier distress of pregnancy or the distress of rearing the child. The third point is that when the whole situation is taken into account, including the status of the fetus, it is very hard to see abortion as the compassionate response. It is seen as compassionate only when the fetus himself is omitted from the picture—when one focuses exclusively on the suffering of the mother. When everything is seen in perspective, the compassionate response is one which is directed towards the well-being of the mother and her baby. And indeed, the major part of this response will be to help the mother to see her baby as *her* baby and as having a special claim on her love and care. In this way, there is a real chance of bringing good out of evil. To terminate the pregnancy would be to add evil to evil, to answer one act of injustice by another.

Fortunately, rape is a comparatively rare occurrence (though, obviously, there are more cases than get reported) and rape-induced pregnancy is still rarer. But if abortion cannot be justified in the case of rape, it obviously cannot be justified in other cases where the distress of the mother is the motivating factor. Nor, *a fortiori*, can it be justified when the abortion is sought for reasons of personal or domestic convenience ('I don't want to lose my job', 'We would have to find a larger house', 'I can't face disturbed nights again' etc.). Nor, again, can it be justified when the mother is unmarried or still at school. In all such cases, natural justice requires that the life of the fetus be protected and that the problems of pregnancy and child-rearing be solved, as best they can, in a way that is compatible with such protection. However, there is one type of case, that of the severely handicapped fetus, which raises issues of a quite different kind, where it may be thought that an abortion could be justified *out of consideration for the child himself*. Thus we may think we know, from tests conducted during the pregnancy, that the severity of the handicap is such that, if the baby were allowed to survive, he would face a great deal of suffering, without sufficient happiness to compensate it. On this basis, it might be claimed, we are doing the baby a good turn by aborting him. We are preventing him from having a life which it is not in his interest to live. Of course, the motive for aborting the handicapped need not be entirely consideration for the fetus himself. The burden to others, both his parents and society at large, may also influence the decision. But since my case against abortion is that it does a grave injustice to the fetus and since the charge of injustice cannot be met by appealing to the beneficial consequences to others, I shall focus exclusively on the claim that abortion may be justified as something in the interests of the person it destroys. At its strongest, it might be claimed that we would be doing the handicapped fetus an injustice by allowing it to live.

The first thing to remember, in discussing this case, is that many people who were born with severe handicaps still achieve a great deal of happiness and fulfilment, and, despite the suffering, are glad to be alive. Moreover, many of them have enriched the lives of others by the courage they have shown in the face of adversity, and they have inspired others with disabilities to face up to their problems in a positive way. Indeed, although suffering is, in itself, an evil and one which we should do what we can (within the limits of morality) to alleviate, there is no denying that, as something to be transcended and overcome, it has contributed to the richness and significance of human life, both to the sufferer and to those involved with him. Of course, there are cases where suffering seems to destroy the human spirit— cases where it seems, in human terms, that the sufferer would, for his own sake and that of others, be better off dead. But even if euthanasia were the right solution for such cases—and I do not think that it is—this would not provide any justification for abortion. For, during the pregnancy, there is no reliable way of telling how much suffering the handicapped person will face and absolutely no indication of how he will respond to it. Are we to abort all babies with a severe physical handicap just to avoid those cases—I suspect a minority—in which the subsequent life would not be, by ordinary standards, worth living? To do so would be an outrageous injustice to those who would, thereby, forfeit lives of happiness and fulfilment.

This point alone is enough to undermine the abortionist's argument. But there are also two further and more fundamental objections. The first of these objections turns on the difference between the following two claims:

(1) Given that someone's future life would not be worth living, it is in his interests to die.
(2) Given the knowledge that someone's future life would not be worth living, we are morally justified in (for his sake) killing him.

The abortionist is implicitly using the truth of (1) as a sufficient basis for asserting (2). But that the basis is insufficient is clearly shown by a different example. Thus suppose, for the sake of argument, that the doctors treating someone with terminal cancer *know* that the remaining months of his life would not be worth living, but that the patient, though aware of the doctors' prognosis, wants to stay alive as long as his illness permits and to receive such medical treatment as is available to ease his condition. It is clear that the doctors do not have the moral right to kill him (of course, they do not have the legal right either) and that to do so, against his wishes, would be nothing short of murder. (Arguably, it is also murder, even if the patient requests it— certainly, it is so legally—but this is not something I need press.) Now, of course, in the case of the handicapped fetus, the wishes of the patient cannot be consulted. Probably the fetus is not sufficiently developed to have a view on the matter, and certainly he cannot express one if he has. But, surely, the correct procedure, for those who advocate euthanasia, would be to defer any action until such time as the patient can make the decision for himself. The fact that the fetus is not in a position to object to being killed does not confer on others the right to kill him. If it did, we would have a similar right to kill an accident victim before he regained consciousness, if we knew that, given his injuries, it was not in his interests to survive. The point, in all these cases, is that, even if someone's life is not worth living, we do not have the moral authority to terminate it without his consent. Nor, in my opinion, do we have the authority to terminate it with his consent, though I shall not try to substantiate that opinion here.

The second objection, which presupposes a Christian (or at least, theistic) viewpoint, concerns the question of what makes a life worth living. Those who claim that it is not in the interests of a severely handicapped fetus to survive are measuring the worth of the future life, to the person himself, in purely mundane and largely hedonistic terms. But, from a Christian viewpoint, the worth of the life depends partly, indeed primarily, on the person's spiritual well-being, which, in turn, depends on his relationship with God. Someone who is severely handicapped may have to forgo many of the ordinary joys of human life and to endure more than the normal share of human suffering. But these things, though misfortunes, do not put him beyond the scope of God's love nor put God beyond the reach of his experience. He still has, as someone created in God's image, a spiritual side to his nature; he is capable of receiving the benefits of God's grace and capable of responding to God with love and worship. And surely we have here, in the communion of man with his Creator, what is of deepest value in human life—indeed, what gives our lives a value, not only here and now, but also in eternity. Thus, if we declare a life as not worth living, because of the quantity of suffering it contains, we are failing to see things in their proper theological perspective. We are assessing the worth of a life in purely mundane terms and taking no account of its deeper spiritual significance.

It might be thought that this second objection does not apply in the case of a severe *mental* handicap. Thus it might be claimed that, in such a case, the handicapped person is incapable of any distinctively human fulfilment, whether mundane or spiritual, and would stand to lose nothing by having his life terminated in the womb.

Even if this claim were correct, it would not help the case for abortion, unless there were a reliable method of assessing during the pregnancy, the extent of the mental retardation. In most cases, we have no such method. Thus we may be able to detect that the fetus is mongoloid (though there can be mistakes here), but we cannot tell how retarded the mongol child will turn out to be. So if we are in the business of extermination (which God forbid), we should at least wait till such time (perhaps when the child is 6 or 7) when we can clearly assess the victim's intellectual capacities. My view, needless to say, is that we should not exterminate him at any time. But, in any case, even if we could, during the pregnancy, accurately assess the extent of the retardation, we have no right to assume that, even in severe cases, the person's future life would be devoid of distinctively human fulfilment. In particular, we have no right to assume that the retarded person does not experience God's love and respond to it. It would be absurd to downgrade the spiritual value of our intellectual capacities. But equally, it is sometimes during periods of intellectual silence that we are most clearly aware of God's presence. How then, can we presume that those in whom, of necessity, the intellect is largely silent have no communion with God?

IV

I have argued that abortion is to be prohibited because it is a grave violation of natural justice. It is to be prohibited for the same reason that any deliberate killing of an innocent human being is to be prohibited because it is, or is morally tantamount to, murder. All this presupposes that human individuals are creatures with a very special intrinsic value, creatures whose lives merit a very special respect. There are those who would dispute this—who would regard human beings as no more than highly developed animals and would assess the value of a human life only in terms of the pleasure it contains and the pleasure it imparts to others. I have already indicated, in discussing the case of the handicapped, that the Christian assessment is quite different, since the Christian sees the nature and value of human life in a theological perspective. I want to end by making explicit what I take to be the three most crucial aspects of this perspective. They are aspects which correspond to the three cardinal doctrines of the Christian faith—the doctrine of creation, the doctrine of the Incarnation and the doctrine of redemption:

(1) Human beings are created by God in his own image. Whatever this means, it clearly separates humans from all other creatures on earth and gives them a special status, as beings who are, in some sense, akin to their Creator.

(2) In Christ, God himself has taken human nature and lived a human life. He has had a human conception, a human birth and a human death. Surely, human nature must be of a very special kind if it is possible for God to assume it and must have a very special significance if God is prepared to assume it.

(3) Not only has God taken human nature, but he was willing for our redemption, to endure, in that nature, the suffering and death of the cross, bearing, in our place, the full consequences of human sin. It is this act of self-sacrifice which, more than anything else, provides a measure of the value which God sets on his human creation. It is a value so great that, for the sake of those thus valued, the omnipotent and self-sufficient Creator of the universe, who stands in need of nothing and is a debtor to no-one, is prepared to take human nature and be crucified.

It is in the perspective of these awesome truths that, as Christians, we must try to grasp the full value of human life and the full enormity of abortion. Humanity is what God has created in his own image, what he has assumed in his Incarnation, and what he has suffered and died to redeem. It is in virtue of these truths that we can properly speak of the sanctity of human life. And it is, in virtue of these truths that we can be quite certain that abortion is not only a violation of natural justice, but an outright rejection of the creative and redemptive purposes of God. Are we to condone the destruction of what God himself has sanctified and has loved at such cost? It is shameful that the question needs to be asked.

3

A Moral—Theological Approach

G. B. BENTLEY

Introductory

Since the function of theology is to provide a signpost to the
knowledge and enjoyment of God, the purpose of *moral* theology,
in the broadest sense of the term, is to show men and women
what they must do in order to attain to that knowledge and
enjoyment. In practice, however, it was found convenient to
divide the subject into two parts in order to make it more
manageable. The treatment of progress in the knowledge and
love of God, and in growth towards what God wills man to
become, came to be known as *ascetic* theology; not because it is
preoccupied with 'asceticism', but because there is, as St Paul
indicated, a certain analogy between the spiritual life and the
training (*askesis*) of an athlete.

Ascetic theology having thus been hived off, so to speak, the
name of *moral* theology was retained by the part that was left,
which thereafter concerned itself, not with progress in spirituality
and sanctity, but with the humbler but very necessary task of
distinguishing right from wrong in human actions. It sought,
among other things, to answer such questions as, "May I do so
and so, or shall I be doing wrong if I do?" and, "Why shouldn't I

do so and so?" It therefore merges into *casuistry*, which is concerned with 'cases of conscience': cases, that is, in which a man finds himself in a dilemma or cannot see how to apply his moral convictions in the particular circumstances he is faced with.

Moral theology in that restricted sense has been much criticized and accused of inculcating a minimum standard of morality instead of pointing towards the heights to be scaled. In practice some works of moral theology have merited that reproach; but critics who think we can do without a discipline that carefully analyses human actions and seeks to draw lines between those which are morally permissible and those which are not are much misguided. It may be that those who have progressed far in responsiveness to the Spirit of God within them and in conformity to the likeness of Christ no longer have need of such a discipline, since they perceive intuitively what they are called upon to do. It may be that for them St Augustine's somewhat cryptic and much abused precept, "Love, and what you will, do", is a safe and adequate guide. But *l'homme moyen sensuel* who is still in the earlier stages of his pilgrimage, as so many of us are, has not yet attained to such perception. The moralists who anticipated Messrs Lennon and McCartney in proclaiming that "All You Need Is Love" can only lead such a man astray, since 'love' is just about the most equivocal and confusing word in the English language and, even when interpreted in the biblical sense of *agape*, denotes a virtue of conation and affection, not of cognition and judgment.

Moral theology does not claim to tell a perplexed individual what he ought to do—that is for his own conscience to decide— but it can help him to sort out the various elements of his problem and clarify the options available; and it may diminish his perplexity by showing him that some action he has been considering is illicit and should be eliminated from his mental debate. Often the elimination of one option makes it easier to choose between the options that remain.

The Constituents of Human Action

One of the most useful achievements of moral theology is its analysis, of human action into the various elements that affect its morality. First and foremost there is 'the thing done'. An action may be described as an expenditure of energy that brings about a change in the *status quo* and comes to an end when the change has been effected. Sometimes an agent may perform an action for the sake of the effect that is intrinsic to it; but often he does what he does not for its own sake, but as a means to some ulterior end that he has in view and that constitutes his motive. In the latter case his objective is not the immediate and intrinsic effect of his action but further consequences that he expects to proceed from it.

Only if the means, that is to say, the thing done, and the ulterior objective are both morally good, is the agent's action wholly blameless. An unworthy intention mars an action that is in itself good. But it is the thing done that is morally crucial. If that is wrong, the most praiseworthy intention cannot make it right; nor can it be justified by appeal to the desirability of the further consequences that are expected to ensue. In other words, the end the agent has in view cannot justify intrinsically evil means. We must not do evil that good may come. This principle needs to be underlined, because it is ignored by a popular kind of utilitarianism which holds that good done to many somehow cancels out injustice done to a few. Caiaphas represented that school of thought when he said, "It is expedient for you that one man should die for the people, and that the whole nation should not perish." One may compare the argument that the atomic bombing of Hiroshima and Nagasaki was justified, because the intention was to scare Japan into surrender by demonstrating the destructive power of the new weapon, and so save the far greater number of lives that would be lost if invasion proved necessary.

There is another factor affecting the morality of an action, namely, the circumstances in which the action is taken. Circumstances may mar an action that is good in itself, but, unlike intention, they can also justify actions that in different circumstances would be wrong. They do that by modifying the intrinsic effect of the thing done. For instance, a surgeon who amputated a perfectly healthy leg would be guilty of mutilating his patient, but, given the circumstance of gangrene, the same action is rightly considered therapeutic rather than destructive. Circumstances have transformed it into an action of mixed effect, partly harmful and partly beneficial, with the benefit clearly outweighing the harm. It is not a case of doing harm in order that benefit may ensue, because one and the same operation both deprives the patient of a leg and removes a grave threat to his whole body. We shall find this principle relevant later when we are considering abortion.

Reasoning in Moral Theology

It should be apparent from what has already been said that, although moral theology is founded on Christian beliefs about God and man, much of the reasoning it uses is ethical rather than theological in character. There is no reason, therefore, why it should not make some contribution to the thinking of those who do not share its Christian presuppositions. It is indeed traditional Christian doctrine that morality is inherent in the nature of man as a rational animal. No esoteric virtue is claimed for the moral precepts found in the Bible, for instance; they are held to be simply reaffirmations of truths we ought to be able to discover for ourselves. That view perhaps needs some revision today, since the growth of human knowledge has made us critical of some biblical dicta. Nevertheless, it is still the case that much of the moral teaching in the Scriptures needs no divine authority to commend it to our consciences. At any rate there will be nothing esoteric about the inquiry into abortion that follows. Appeal to Christian beliefs will be made only in confirmation of conclusions first reached by reasoning.

Human Liberty and Moral Law

It is an axiom of moral theology that "liberty is in possession": that is to say, human freedom of action is logically prior to its restriction by moral prohibitions. There is, therefore, a presumption in favour of freedom to act according to conscience, and the onus is on those who would curtail that freedom by appeal to some contrary law. They must make their case beyond reasonable doubt, for it is another axiom that a doubtful law does not lay an obligation on the conscience.

It is time now to consider the question of abortion. Given the present level of female coital activity, consequent on woman's rediscovery of her natural sexual appetite after its virtual repression over much of society in the nineteenth century, and given also the readiness of many young girls, now that the old stigma has been removed from the sexual act, to welcome coital initiation at the age of thirteen or thereabouts, it is to be expected that situations in which abortion seems to offer the obvious way out of difficulties will occur with considerable frequency. Readily available though it is, contraception is still liable to be neglected or inefficiently practised. Teenagers in particular are apt to be careless of precautions in this as in other matters. To quote one young woman: "At that age you always assume that it can't happen to you."

Let us then postulate a case in which a woman or girl has become pregnant against her will and is appalled by the consequences she foresees, from which she can see no escape if her pregnancy continues. Suppose those close to her press abortion on her, and that impartial counsellors as well think it would be in the best interests of all concerned. There is indeed no denying that in some circumstances the ending of a pregnancy seems highly desirable. One cannot but feel for a woman who (to adapt Tennyson's words) "has that within her womb that leaves her ill content" and is destined, if nothing is done, to bear a child she never intended to have and does not want, perhaps to the serious detriment of her future life.

The question facing the moralist, therefore, is whether in such a case the woman concerned is at liberty to act as seems good to her and to her counsellors, or whether it can be shown beyond reasonable doubt that there is a relevant moral law that she would be breaking if she did.

Is Abortion Homicide?

On the face of it, yes. The object of the act of abortion is summarily to cut short an incipient human life in the belief that it is in the best interests of the pregnant woman and perhaps of others that that life should cease to exist. So the act proposed certainly appears to amount to homicide, and homicide is morally culpable except in circumstances that are not present in the case we are considering. Since it is an act that is evil in itself, no beneficial consequences can make it good.

The view that killing a child in the womb is homicide is challenged however. Killing is not homicide, it is argued, unless the victim is a human being, and is it not straining language to call an embryo or fetus that? The law of the land does not give the name of homicide to killing a child before it has an existence independent of its mother, and the man in the street seems to feel in his bones that there is a great deal of difference between procuring an abortion and killing an infant after birth. In fact, it is a common opinion that the new life developing inside a woman's body is less than fully human to begin with and attains to full humanity only later.

There is a sense in which that opinion is well-founded. It is some time before an embryo begins to look like a human being, and at the outset its specifically human characteristics are still in potentiality, awaiting actualization over a period of years covering postnatal as well as prenatal existence. But it is genetically complete from the time of conception; the potentialities are all there from the beginning; and there is no break in the continuity of its subsequent development. All attempts to locate within the continuum a point of transition from a pre-human to a human condition have been unconvincing.

At one time the 'quickening' was invested with great significance, but now that we know so much more about the activity that goes on in a woman's body from the beginning of the generative process that significance is seen to have been misplaced. The zygote is very much alive, if not kicking, from the time of fertilization. Then, more recently, some have argued that an embryo cannot be called human until neurological activity has begun; but it difficult to understand why such unique importance should be attached to that particular actualization of the genetic programme, since it is only one in a continuing series of such actualizations.

The only transition that can be identified with any certainty is that of birth, when the infant exchanges its original environment in the womb for another outside and ceases to rely on the life-support system in its mother's body. A former archbishop, now no longer with us, maintained in correspondence with the present writer that that was the point at which it became recognizably a human person with an identity distinct from its mother's and was fully invested with the human right to life. There is a bluff common sense about the late prelate's opinion that has its attractions. Moreover, as we have noted, the man in the street is apt to feel much the same. To the male a child is scarcely a reality until he sees it. A mother, on the other hand, comes to know her baby before it is born, and the experience of delivery leaves no room for doubt that the creature brought forth is identical with the creature she had long known and felt moving within her. To her the theory of 'humanization by birth' cannot be anything but nonsense; she knows that delivery has simply changed her child's environment, not the child itself.

The fact of the matter is that attempts to distinguish between a pre-human stage and the fully human stage in the unbroken development of a child are thoroughly misguided and as unreliably speculative as medieval attempts to identify a point at which a rational soul was 'infused'. Being the fruit of the copulation of two members of the species *homo sapiens*, the zygote cannot but belong to the same species. What other species could it assigned to? The organism generated by the union of human sperm with human ovum cannot be anything but a human being 'in embryo'. Genetically, complete from the time of conception, it is programmed as a human being and nothing else. Like all living beings, it has to grow and develop before it reaches maturity, but there is no point at which it can be killed without cutting short a human life. It follows that abortion has the nature of homicide, though the law does not give it that name. So moral theology cannot offer the unwillingly pregnant woman escape from her predicament by means of early abortion before her child becomes 'human' and acquires human rights.

The difference so many of us feel to exist between killing a child in the womb and killing a child after birth is mainly subjective. While we have a clear mental image of an infant after birth—an image that may well have emotive associations—our notion of a child in the womb is liable to be inchoate and vague in the extreme. Until comparatively recently most people knew far too little about its appearance and behaviour to form any picture of it at all, still less to appreciate its continuity and coherence with the infant after birth. Our ignorance is being lessened nowadays, but it will still take some time for imagination to catch up with the reality.

God and the Life in the Womb

Up to now there has not been occasion to introduce any specifically Judaeo-Christian beliefs into the discussion, but at this point we must refer briefly to Christian doctrine concerning the 'special relationship' of the Creator of his human creatures. God, it is believed, has created the human race for familiar friendship with himself, intending that men and women should be 'divinized' by his own Spirit and so enabled to become to him as sons and daughters to their father. If that is true, then every human child conceived is a potential child of God and, as such, is known and cherished by him. Every child belongs to God and is under his protection. If so, it is inconceivable that his care for each child should not be effective from the very beginning; and indeed the Bible affirms that it is so effective. In Psalm 139, for instance:

> Thou it was who didst fashion my inward parts;
> thou didst knit me together in my mother's womb.
>
> Thou knowest me through and through:
>   my body is no mystery to thee,
> how I was secretly kneaded into shape
>   and patterned in the depths of the earth.
> Thou didst see my limbs unformed in the womb,
>   and in thy book they are all recorded;
> day by day they were fashioned,
>   not one of them was late in growing.

Incidentally, it is worth noting that the Psalmist finds it natural to use the first-personal pronoun of his prenatal existence. We should all probably do the same, if we had occasion to talk about our lives before birth. It would not enter our heads that 'I' might not have been 'I' from the very beginning.

Then there is Jeremiah 1.5:

> Before I formed you in the womb I knew you for my own;
> before you were born I consecrated you, I appointed you a
> prophet to the nations.

God is said also to have had a similar 'special relationship' with John the Baptist before he was burnt, and to have caused Mary to conceive Jesus by the "overshadowing" of his Spirit. Thus to

Christians, destruction of life in the womb should be not merely homicide—not merely killing an embryo member of the human species—but cutting off a life already known and loved by God and intended for familiar friendship with him. The moral objections to abortion do not, of course, depend on Christian belief, but it reinforces them.

Keeping on the Safe Side

It would be disingenuous to give the impression that all moral theologians have always agreed that an embryo is a human being with all human rights from the time of conception. On the contrary, there have always been some to argue that, although, of course, belonging to the species *homo sapiens*, it does not immediately become a 'person' with the same right to life as a child after birth. St Thomas Aquinas, for one, held that until animated by the rational soul about six weeks after conception it was still of an animal nature. That did not mean that it was fair game for abortion until the close season opened at the end of the six weeks, but that during that period its claim to life might possibly yield to some greater claim.

All such speculations are, in the nature of the case, bound to remain unproven. This is the point, therefore, where another principle of moral theology needs to be introduced. In most everyday matters, when an agent has a moral choice to make and finds himself unable to reach certainty about his duty, it is generally allowed that he will not show himself to be morally irresponsible if he acts on probability: if, that is to say, there seem to him to be sound reasons for doing what he elects to do, even though he can think of sound reasons for taking the other option. But when it is a matter of life and death that confronts him, he has not the same liberty; he is bound to choose what seems to him the safer course. That means, in the matter we are considering, that even if it were shown to be highly probable that Aquinas was right in his speculation, an agent would still not be justified in acting on it. The embryo must be given the benefit of the slightest doubt and its life be protected. The same rule is applicable to other speculations and theories about the status of life in the womb. Later on we shall be examining the possibility that the embryo's right to life can be overridden by some other right, but the arguments will not turn on speculations about its status.

A Woman's Rights over her Body

There is another approach to the question of the right to life of an unborn child. Even if life in the womb is to be regarded as human from the first, does not the fact that it exists within and is attached to the pregnant woman's body modify its status importantly? Indeed, since the child *en ventre sa mère* (in his mother's womb) has, so to speak, grown out of her flesh, and is totally dependent on her body for its life, should it not be regarded as part of that body?

It seems that the ancients did not regard it, and their view of the matter is not wholly unknown today. Suppose for a moment that it is a just view; it follows that a woman has the same rights over the organism in her womb as over the rest of her body. Suppose further, that its presence in her proves burdensome, offensive or dangerous to her; is she not entitled to have it removed in the same way as a bothersome or dangerous growth? Since it is an unwelcome intruder into her body, its humanity—if on this view it can be regarded as human—cannot override her right to rid her body of anything that causes her distress.

As we shall see later, where danger is concerned a woman's right to protect herself can indeed, in certain circumstances, override the right to life of an embryo or fetus, but not on the ground that the organism in her womb is part of her body. The opinion that it *is* part cannot be upheld. As soon as an ovum has been fertilized it becomes quite evidently a distinct centre of life and movement. The purposive journey of the zygote to find a suitable place in which to settle itself is enough to show that it is distinct, with a life of its own, even though it cannot survive for long without attaching itself to the maternal life-support system. It 'uses' the body within which it has been conceived for safe lodging and sustenance; and the womb accepts its activity and readily permits it to become attached, but does not assimilate it. The distinct centre of life remains.

Nowadays a woman's rights over her body are wont to be asserted very emphatically. It is claimed that she is entitled to be sole arbiter of whether to bear a child or not. Even when allowance has been made for a measure of rhetorical hyperbole this claim proves on examination to be rather obscure. Its import appears to depend on the social background against which it is made. In the days before the general spread of contraception it would probably have meant that a woman had an inalienable right to decide whether or not to admit male penetration and ejaculation and would have amounted to repudiation of the received doctrine that the marriage covenant involved a mutual transfer of rights over the body. Today it could mean that in copulation it is the woman's prerogative to decide whether contraception is to be used or not. But the context in which the claim is usually made suggests that that is not what is intended. More probably it asserts that, if a woman finds herself pregnant, she, and she alone, is entitled to decide whether the pregnancy shall go full term or be prematurely terminated.

It is not made clear what the basis of this claim is, apart from the fact that the woman is the only person immediately affected by the pregnancy, and by giving birth, if the pregnancy is allowed to continue; but in effect it appears to be not very different from the assumption that the organism in a woman's womb is part of her body—an assumption that has already been discussed and rejected. It should be noted, however, that this modern claim ascribes to a woman an absolute sovereignty over her body that is subject to question. It is a long-standing principle in both morals and medicine that no part of the human body should be destroyed unless its destruction is necessary for the health of the body as a whole. Destroying a perfectly healthy embryo or fetus simply because the pregnant woman decides not to have a child is, apart from any other considerations, forbidden by that principle.

It is understandable that women who have grown up with contraception and the two types of copulation, generative and non-generative, that contraception has established, should suppose that they have a right to the latter type, and that if an 'accident' occurs, they are entitled to rectify it by abortion. But that is a misunderstanding of the situation that contraception has created. We are not, of course, concerned here with the moral acceptability of contraception, but only with the effect it has had on the sexual act and on attitudes to it. That act combines two principal functions. On the one hand it reunites the two sexes into which humanity has been divided into a single androgynous organism. In biblical terminology it makes a man and a woman 'one flesh'. That takes place on the carnal level, but it can subserve total personal union if that is what the man and woman involved are seeking. On the other hand it simultaneously fertilizes the woman, if the time is ripe for fertilization.

Without contraception it is impossible to separate the two functions, except in so far as a couple can make use of infertile periods in the female cycle. What contraception has done, therefore, is to enable a couple to enjoy the unitive, or, in ethological language, 'bonding' function without activating the impregnatory; and, since family planning is now generally accepted as desirable, the non-generative act has come to be regarded as the norm and the potentially generative as reserved for occasions when procreation is deliberately intended. In other words, contraception is maintained most of the time and abandoned only on the comparatively few occasions when offspring is desired.

Contraception has also made copulation available to relationships where no procreation is desired and would indeed be considered irresponsible, and has facilitated fornication.

In these circumstances it is, as has been said, understandable that non-generative copulation should have come to be regarded as a right; but that view of the matter involves a misconception of what contraception does. It does not alter the nature of the sexual act and make it non-generative. Structurally the act remains inseminatory; all contraception does is to impede impregnation, either by putting a barrier between the seed and its natural destination, or by making the female body unresponsive to the seed. If then it fails in its object, so that the act reverts to its natural condition, and conception ensues the couple concerned may complain of their contraceptive or deplore their inefficient use of it, but they are not entitled to complain of nature and revenge themselves on it by killing the new life it has produced. The truth is that, albeit unwittingly and unintentionally, they used the means to generation and reaped what they sowed. Their intention does not alter the nature of the act they in fact performed.

This is an important truth that is too often forgotten. There is a certain irresponsibility about copulating with contraception if those concerned fail entirely to face the possibility of conception ensuing and are not prepared to accept the consequences if it does. One can understand that this is a very hard saying for those who regard contraception as their licence to 'screw around', but we should consider the foreseeable consequences of our actions, even unlikely ones, and be prepared to accept them if they occur.

It follows that, if it makes sense to say a woman has a 'right' not to bear a child, she surrenders it when she admits male penetration and ejaculation, even if contraception is employed.

So-called 'Therapeutic' Abortion

Although the fact that an embryo or fetus is contained within and attached to a woman's body does not entitle her to destroy it at will, it nevertheless has important moral significance. For instance, medical or surgical treatment that a pregnant woman needs for her own welfare cannot be given without affecting the life in her womb in some measure, and in some cases it may entail its destruction. Thus a pregnant woman found to suffer from carcinoma of the uterus cannot be given the hysterectomy she urgently needs, and to which she has a right, without causing the death of the child growing within her. These are just the kind of circumstances in which the principle of double or mixed effect, referred to above, is applicable. It is a principle that is applied regularly by physicians and surgeons, though they may not think of it in those terms. As the press keeps reminding us, many medicines that doctors prescribe have mixed effects or, to use the current language, have harmful side-effects that are inseparable from their therapeutic action. If doctors were required to prescribe only what was exclusively beneficial, they would be denied the use of much of the pharmacopoeia. As it is, however, the principle of double effect permits them to prescribe what is known to be harmful as well as beneficial, provided always that the foreseen harmful effects do not outweigh the expected benefit to their patients and can credibly be called 'side-effects' of what is predominantly therapeutic.

At first sight it may seem irresponsible to treat so destructive an effect as the ending of a human life as a 'side-effect'. Although the intention of performing a hysterectomy would be to save the woman and not to kill the fetus, what is done looks very like saving one life at the expense of another. It must be borne in mind, however, that the fetus is doomed in any case. The cancer threatens both lives, and only the woman's can be saved. In normal circumstances she has a right to whatever therapy she needs, and that right is not overridden because the necessary therapy cannot be given without hastening the end of another life that is bound to be lost even if no action is taken. The woman's claim to remedial treatment can be met, and ought to be.

Though it would be disputed by many moral theologians, the opinion of the present writer is that the principle of double effect is applicable also to cases, nowadays happily very rare, in which continuance of a pregnancy is itself a serious danger to the woman concerned. Often the term 'termination of pregnancy' is used as an euphemism for deliberate and direct abortion, but in the circumstances we are considering it accurately describes the remedy that the welfare of the woman requires. The object of the action she needs is not killing the fetus, for that in itself would not benefit the woman at all, but simply and solely an emptying of her womb. Could that be achieved without kiling the fetus, it would be. Emptying the womb is not wrong in itself; when a fetus is viable, and hastening delivery is in the woman's interests, no question is raised about premature emptying. It is the circumstance that the fetus is not yet capable of surviving outside the womb that turns emptying the womb into an action of mixed effect. If consequent death of the fetus may be regarded as an unwanted but unavoidable side-effect of a legitimate procedure.

Some writers have suggested that where pregnancy is a serious threat to the life or health of the woman concerned, the fetus may be regarded as an 'aggressor', albeit an involuntary one, and that the woman is entitled to defend herself against the aggression. The analogy seems rather far-fetched. One may say that the woman invited the fetus to take up residence in her womb and it has not in any way exceeded the terms of the invitation. It has not 'turned nasty'. However, it is true that in the circumstances the effect of its presence in her body is in some respects analogous to that of a growth.

Homicidal Abortion

In the kind of case we have been considering, the death of the fetus is not willed for its own sake, nor is it the means to the end in view. What is willed is evacuation of the womb as the means of safeguarding the welfare of the woman, and the death of the fetus is an unavoidable side-effect of that because the fetus is not yet able to survive outside the womb.

The case is entirely different when pregnancy is not dangerous to the woman and the object of terminating it is not to empty the womb but, to put it bluntly, to get rid of the child. The action taken is, in fact, homicidal and does not essentially differ from infanticide. There can be no appeal in this case to the principle of double effect. To claim that the death of the fetus is an unavoidable side-effect of an innocent action would be arrant hypocrisy, for getting rid of the fetus is the very essence of what is done. If any good, in fact, comes of it, that is not an intrinsic effect of the action, which is wholly destructive, but only a contingent consequence—one of the ripples spreading from the place where the stone fell in. If the killing is done for the sake of such consequence, it is a case of doing evil that good may come.

Abortion after Rape

A pregnancy resulting from rape needs further consideration. It differs from other pregnancies in that it is an effect integral to an act of grave injustice. The rape was an act of aggression and the presence in the victim's womb of the effect of it is a prolongation of it. In this case, therefore, the embryo can reasonably be regarded as an aggressor continuing the aggression of the rapist, whose genes it carries.

Other injuries inflicted on the victim's body by the rapist are given remedial treatment as a matter of course; must the greatest and most lasting injury of all be left alone and allowed to perpetuate the injustice? Surely it is an aggravation of the injustice to require a woman who has been sexually assaulted to protect and bring to birth, and perhaps afterwards nurture and care for, the offspring of her assailant. Having failed to repel his assault, must she now be content to let the fruits of his victory over her life and grow inside her body? It seems intolerable that his genes should be allowed to benefit from his violence, and that she should be under obligation to foster their survival. To say that she must put up with their presence in her, simply because she was not strong enough, or well enough trained in self-defence, or had not rendered herself impregnable by contraception, is rather like saying that a landowner is entitled to resist invasion of his property so long as the invader remains outside the boundary fence, but that once the fence has been breached and the invader has occupied his territory, he is not only debarred from trying to eject him, but is bound to give him shelter and sustenance. That simply does not make sense.

The objection to abortion in such a case is that the embryo occupying the victim's body cannot be held responsible for the invasion that put it there. Indeed, in view of the unhappy circumstances of its conception, it too is a victim of its father's wrongdoing. Nevertheless the fact remains that its conception was part and parcel of the sexual assault, so that it too is an unjust intruder. The victim, having failed to repel the initial invasion of her body, that is to say, penetration and insemination, must surely be entitled to take steps afterwards to nullify the effects, including conception if it ensues. As for the embryo, the sin of the father is visited on his child and deprives it of its right to life.

That, at least, is the conclusion of the present writer. Other moralists are of a different opinion, it must be confessed.* It has also to be admitted that, from the point of view of the law, rape is so difficult to establish with certainty that licensing abortion on that ground alone would have its dangers.

The Case of Abnormality

A provision of the existing law, that permits abortion when there is good reason to believe that a child would be born seriously deformed or with other grave abnormality, is surely extremely questionable. It can be defended on utilitarian principles, of course, on the ground that cutting short the life of any notably defective child is best for all concerned: for the mother and the family, for society, and, some would argue, for the child itself. It is true that the birth of gravely abnormal children does impose heavy burdens on mothers, families and society, and one can

★ See p. 46

understand and sympathize with the distress of those closely concerned when the likelihood of abnormality is conveyed to them. But we must not destroy human lives because their existence puts heavy burdens on us. If that were permissible the world would be littered with corpses!

As for the contention that it is better for some human beings not to exist than to exist, it can hardly be taken seriously. Existence is itself a good, for all other goods depend on it. And which of us is competent to decide for another that his life is not worth living? It is surely the height of presumption to make such a decision for a person who in the nature of the case cannot be consulted and has not yet had the opportunity to experience living in the world. The presumption is compounded by the fact that, when abortion is resorted to, no one can claim to have exact knowledge of the condition in which the child will be born. If killing the unfit is considered to be morally legitimate, would it not be better to wait until the candidate has been born and its abnormalities can be more accurately assessed?

Another possible argument should perhaps be noticed. Let it be supposed that Nature when aiming at making a human being sometimes fails to achieve her purpose. Suppose further that miscarriage is her way of disposing of the imperfect attempts. Now gynaecological advances prevent many miscarriages and so preserve Nature's failures as well as her successes. Is it not desirable and permissible in these circumstances for gynaecology to do what Nature would probably have done but for its intervention?

Unfortunately we have not yet perfected a sure means of determining when, if ever, a fetus is not simply a defective human being but falls short of being a human being at all. So, once again, any decision we made would be intolerably presumptuous; and if we implemented it we should be transgressing the rule of choosing the safer course in matters of life and death.

Those who accept Christian beliefs about the purpose of God for his human creatures have a further point to make. As they see it, the deformed and abnormal are "known of God" like other men and loved by him, and are within the scope of his purpose. Obviously deformity does not prevent a person from coming to know and love God and inherit the kingdom of heaven; and it may well be that those whose mental defects impede their converse with men can become children of God and enjoy familiar converse with him. So although to those who have been spared such afflictions the lives of those with grave disabilities may seem to be not worth living, those lives are their opportunity to attain to life eternal.

IUD and 'the morning-after Pill'

These are not contraceptives, though often represented as such, but methods of procuring very early abortion; for they act after conception, not before. Contraception works either by rendering a woman temporarily sterile or by preventing the seed from reaching the ova; the methods under consideration work by ' "putting a spoke in the wheel" after fertilization', as one writer has put it. The consequence is that the zygote is prevented from carrying out its programme and securing implantation in the womb.

There is a certain analogy between the operation of the intra-uterine device and the ancient practice of 'exposing' unwanted infants, in that in both cases the organism is separated from the environment it needs for survival and growth. The exposed infant, however, was in better case than the impeded zygote, since there was a chance that it might be found and nurtured by someone else.

Recent embryology, however, has come up with an interesting finding. We are told that the zygote remains mobile in the fallopian tube and the womb for from seven to twelve days after conception before implantation in the wall of the uterus, and that until implantation has been completed, and possibly even for a day or two after, division into identical twins is still possible. There is also some evidence to the effect that in this early stage one human being may be formed by the fusion of two fertilized ova. On the strength of this some theologians have argued that, so long as the possibility of division or fusion remains, a zygote cannot be regarded as an individual, and that therefore IUD and other means of preventing implantation do not constitute abortion.

Although the present writer would be glad to be able to avail himself of that argument, he regretfully finds it unconvincing.

Even if a zygote has not yet 'decided' whether to be one person or two, there is no question but that it is incipient human life and so entitled to protection. In fact, if a zygote has the possibility of growing into two human persons, not one only, the importance of preserving its life is all the greater.

Although the embryological findings may be correct, the interpretation put upon them is only speculative and, in view of the principle of being on the safe side, does not provide a sure enough basis for action. In any case, all the attempts to identify a period in human life that is *not* human look like special pleading. One cannot get away from the fact that the zygote contains in itself all the elements, in an as yet undeveloped form, of a mature human being. It is genetically complete from the time of conception and needs no extraneous addition to complement it. All it requires for actualization of its potentiality is to be let alone to live and grow in the environment that is natural to it. No matter how early we wield the chopper, we are killing not just a zygote, but the person who is to be. Human life must be protected from its very beginning, or it is not protected at all.

Postscript

In this essay we have had necessarily to confine our attention to the sort of question that arises in our own society and societies akin to it. We have not been able to consider at all the societies in which steeply rising birth rates threaten national diaster. Had we been able to, there would, of course, have been no fundamental difference in our treatment of abortion, but we should have had to go on to consider whether the morality of it was at all affected by the claims of 'necessity' and 'the public good', taking into account the maxims *Necessitas non habet legem* (Necessity has no law) and *Salus populi suprema lex* (The good of the people is the highest law). Necessity and the public good are very difficult concepts to handle, but in some circumstances they cannot be ignored.

As far as our own society is concerned, although, as has already been said, a moral theologian has no wish to circumscribe human liberty of choice unnecessarily, when human life is at stake he can do no other than uphold its claim to protection and reaffirm the intrinsic evil of homicide. While sympathizing with those for whom unintended and unwanted pregnancy has created intractable problems he can only say to them that some other solution than abortion must somehow be found.

The Christian Witness

4

Using the Bible in the Debate about Abortion

J. W. ROGERSON

"Go buy the book and then go by the book" is a successful slogan used by the United Bible Societies to promote the circulation and reading of the Bible. Excellent though the slogan is, it fails to indicate that "going by the book" is not always a straightforward matter. In the probably apocryphal story about a person who was seeking guidance from the Bible and who turned up in succession a passage about Judas hanging himself and the command, "Go and do thou likewise", we see the dangers of random text selection at their greatest. Unfortunately, this does not prevent people from plucking texts out of their context, and applying them to contemporary social issues without regard to what these texts meant in their original setting, and whether they can be legitimately applied to the modern world.

Fortunately, in the case of the debate about abortion, there are no texts that can be simply applied to the matters. The Bible does not directly mention abortion anywhere. However, this does not prevent the misuse of passages that are thought to indicate a pro-life stance in the Bible, and there is a danger that over-zealous advocates of the pro-life viewpoint may damage their cause by using the Bible in ways likely to be repugnant to people who are not hard-line fundamentalists. Examples of this misuse will be provided later. In the first instance, it will be useful to outline what is known about pregnancy and birth practices in biblical times.

In the standard versions of the Bible, it is often stated that a woman conceived.[1] Of course, this does not relate in any way to the modern medical understanding of conception. The biblical writers knew nothing about fertilization, but they knew about women's periods (which made women "unclean" while they lasted)[2] and about the best times for achieving pregnancy through sexual intercourse. Strictly speaking, the Hebrew and Greek phrases translated as (she) conceived ought to be rendered 'become pregnant'.

This is, in fact the rendering found in *The Translator's New Testament* for Matthew 1:23: 'A maiden will become pregnant and bear a son, and they will name him Emmanuel.'[3] The signs of the onset of pregnancy having been recognized, precautions were taken to prevent injury to the unborn child that might arise through the mother attempting heavy manual jobs. The evidence for this is not in the Bible, but in later Jewish writings.[4] If it is fair to reckon back from these to biblical times, we can also say that many superstitions would be affected by the eating and living habits of the mother.[5] What is not clear is whether the unborn child was thought of as a person.

The Old Testament gives several passages in which the growth of the unborn child is described. Unfortunately for our purposes, these passages are in poetry, and we cannot be sure whether they represent what the biblical writers actually thought was happening inside the womb. Job 10:10 asks the rhetorical question: 'Didst thou not pour me out like milk and curdle me like cheese?' It continues: 'Thou didst clothe me with skin and flesh and knit me together with bones and sinews.'

The reference to curdling may reflect the fact that as a result of miscarriages and premature births, the biblical writers were aware of the difference between the fetus in an undeveloped state, and in a state where the outward form of the child was already complete.[6]

The other main passage which speaks of the growth of the child in the womb is found in Psalm 139:13-16.

> For thou didst form my inward parts,
>   thou didst knit me together in my mother's womb.
>
> I praise thee, for thou art fearful and wonderful.
>   Wonderful are thy works!
>   Thou knowest me right well;
>
> My frame was not hidden from thee,
>   when I was made in secret,
>   intricately wrought in the depths of the earth.
>
> Thy eyes beheld my unformed substance;
>   in thy book were written, every one of them,
>   the days that were formed for me, when as yet there was
>   none of them.

In this passage, the stress is again upon the growth of the child from something formless (verse 16) to something developed and complete. It is clear that the psalmist, like Job, believed that God was intimately involved in this process of growth and development. Whether this point is of relevance to the modern debate about abortion must be considered later.

Before the proper time for birth, "natural abortions" could occur, and Job, lamenting the fact that he was born at all asks, 'Why was I not as a hidden untimely birth, as infants that never see the light?[7]' The addition of the word "hidden" to the Hebrew word translated "untimely birth" most likely indicates that such "untimely births" were immediately disposed of, and not shown to family or neighbours.

For birth itself, it is likely that the mother adopted a squatting position, and that the infant was received onto the knees of the midwife.[8] Thus Job complained, 'Why did the knees receive me?' Exodus 1:16 mentions a birthstool—possibly something on which the mother sat, with an opening to enable the child to pass from the womb and to be taken by the midwife.[9]

That abortion was known, practised and punished in the ancient Near East is evident from the Middle Assyrian Laws, where we read:

> If a woman has had a miscarriage by her own act, when they
> have presented her (and) convicted her, they shall impale
> her on stakes without burying her. If she died in having the
> miscarriage, they shall impale her on stakes without
> burying her. If someone hid that woman when she had the
> miscarriage (without) informing (the king) ...[10]

The text breaks off, but it is a safe deduction that the laws pres-
cribed penalties for those who aided abortions.

It is difficult to know what to conclude from the complete
silence of biblical law on the subject. Arguments from silence are
always open to being stood on their head. However, the view that
will be taken here is that the silence indicates that abortion was
not commonly practised, if at all, in ancient Israel. This tentative
conclusion can be justified by the following considerations.

(a) It is known that exposure of unwanted female children took
place. This is clear from Ezekiel 16:4, where God speaks of
finding Jerusalem as one might find an exposed infant girl:

> Your navel string was not cut, nor were you washed with
> water to cleanse you, nor rubbed with salt, nor swathed
> with bands. No eye pitied you, to do any of these things to
> you out of compassion for you, but you were cast out on the
> open field, for you were abhorred, on the day that you were
> born.

Since it is clear that male children were much to be desired in
ancient Israel,[11] it is likely that pregnancies were not interfered
with, lest a male child be lost. Exposure of unwanted children,
almost certainly females, although no doubt regarded as a serious
crime (in fact, Old Testament law is silent in this matter also),
had the advantages of preventing the danger of death that might
occur to the mother because of the abortion, and of keeping the
options open in case a male child was to be born.

(b) Old Testament penalties for adultery, fornication and incest
were extremely severe, usually involving the death penalty. The
husband had far-reaching powers if he even *suspected* adultery on
the part of his wife,[12] and thus it may well be that few situations
existed outside wedlock in which an abortion would be necessary. It is true that the Old Testament contains a word (*mamzer*)
usually translated "bastard" at one of its two occurrences,

Deuteronomy 23:2. 'No bastard shall enter the assembly of the LORD.' However, the meaning of the word is disputed. A majority viewpoint is that it refers to a child born of an incestuous union. If this is correct, then we must suppose that if the death penalty was enforced for incest, this was delayed until the birth of the child. If we could be sure that the *mamzer* was a child from an incestuous relationship who had been allowed to be born before his parents were executed, this would be of considerable importance for the discussion about abortion. However, in the light of the uncertainties involved, the point can not be pressed.[13]

A passage that has attracted some attention, since it appears to bear upon how the unborn child was regarded in the Old Testament, is in Exodus 21:22-24. The law envisages a pregnant woman getting hurt in a fight between two men (perhaps she goes to the aid of her husband), and having a miscarriage as a result. If "harm" follows, the penalty is in accordance with *talion*—life for life, eye for eye, etc. If there is no harm, the man causing the injury is fined. Unfortunately, it is not clear whether the "harm" refers to harm done to the woman or to her prematurely-born child. The most natural interpretation is that the harm refers to the woman. It would be a very harsh law indeed that put to death a man who unintentionally caused a miscarriage early in a woman's pregnancy. Presumably, the antagonist would take particular care if the woman's pregnancy was obviously well advanced. However, distinguished advocacy has been put forward on behalf of the view that the guilty man will be punished for injury caused to the *prematurely-born child*, and if this is the correct interpretation, it suggests that unborn children were highly regarded in ancient Israel.[14]

The discussion so far has shown what ought to be obvious in any case, but what is, in fact, overlooked time and again, that the Bible presupposes a social and cultural situation totally different from that which obtains today. If I am correct in assuming that abortion is not prohibited in the Bible because it was not commonly practised, this only goes to point up the difference between ancient Hebrew and Jewish society where children were generally desired, and our own over-populated world where abortions can be numbered in millions. Faced with this cultural difference, a possible conclusion could be drawn that the Bible has no place in the modern discussion, and is best left out. This is not a view that I share; but at the same time, I must also say that I find it difficult to agree with some of the arguments commonly put forward in support of the pro-life position on the basis of the Bible. These will now be considered.

It is often asserted that the Bible as a whole has a strong pro-life orientation, and that it forbids the taking of life. Two texts in particular are cited:

> Whoever sheds the blood of man,
> by man shall his blood be shed;
> for God made man in his own image (Genesis 9:6)

and, 'You shall not kill' (Exodus 20:13). It is not my intention to deny the importance of these passages. However, the argument that the Bible is pro-life will hardly satisfy the uncommitted, if no attempt is made to deal with those parts of the Old Testament in which God commands the killing of men, women and children. Thus, we read in Joshua 10:40 that Joshua 'utterly destroyed all that breathes, as the LORD God of Israel commanded'. Again, in 1 Samuel 15:2, God commands Saul to smite the Amalekites: 'Do not spare them, but kill both man and woman, infant and suckling ...' No doubt it can be said that the Amalekites were being punished because they opposed the Israelites on their way out of Egypt; but sensitive modern readers can be forgiven for doubting whether they should take any notice of a book which contains such crude notions of corporate responsibility, even if our modern so-called civilized society has perfected violent forms of retaliation that do not discriminate between the innocent and the guilty.

My own approach to passages such as those in Joshua 10:40 and 1 Samuel 15:2 is that we must recognize frankly that the conventions of ancient war did allow for whole communities to be "devoted" to the god, and thus to be completely wiped out. The belief of Israelites, in the early stages of their history, that their God wished them to "devote" people to him was sincere, but mistaken. On the other hand, it is clear from recent scholarship that the passages which speak of this wholesale slaughter reached their present form during or after the exile (6th century B.C.) In their final form, they were not intended primarily to be commands to exterminate enemies, but rather to be object lessons about the ills that befell the Israelites when they turned to the gods of the peoples alongside whom they lived.

Another common appeal from the Bible in support of the pro-life position urges that according to the Bible, human life begins at conception.[15] There are several difficulties here. First, it has already been pointed out that the Bible knows nothing of conception in the modern medical sense. Second, we cannot be *certain* that the life of the unborn child was regarded as sacrosanct in the Bible. We *can* be sure that at least the writer of Job and the author of Psalm 139 believed that God was intimately involved in the growth of the unborn child, and it would not be unreasonable to appeal to this fact in the abortion debate. Indeed, this sense of God's involvement in the process of growth seems to be taken to the point where it is asserted that he is responsible also for the handicaps with which people are born. Thus, in Exodus 4:11, the rhetorical question is addressed to Moses:

> Who has made man's mouth?
> Who makes him dumb, or deaf, or seeing, or blind?
> Is it not I, the LORD?

Yet this last point only reveals another difficulty. Ignoring the fact that people who are not hard-line fundamentalists will find it difficult to take literally statements about God's *direct* participation in the growth of unborn children, there is no doubt that they will find repugnant the assertion that God is responsible for the handicaps of handicapped children. Are we to suppose that thalidomide victims were somehow God's intended results? Why did Jesus combat evil in the form of physical handicap, and regard it as part of the kingdom of Satan?[16] If doctors and surgeons work to help handicapped people overcome their handicaps, are they defying the will of God? Further, if unborn children begin to develop in the wrong parts of the mother's body, thus necessitating a termination of pregnancy in the sense defined by Mr. Norris, is not this an interference in the activity of God who has supposedly placed the child where it is?

Another line of approach appeals to texts in which individuals are named who are called before birth. Among these are Jeremiah, in Jeremiah 1:5, the prince of the five names in Isaiah

9:1-6, and our Lord in Matthew 1:21. In the Old Testament examples, we must be clear what can and what cannot be proved. Even if it is accepted that Jeremiah and the prince were "people" before their birth in God's sight, it does not follow that this is true of all mankind. We have noted that the Old Testament writers were familiar with so-called natural abortions. In these cases, had God named or called them before their birth? If so, why did they not live? If not, can we assert that every person is known to God before his birth?

The case of our Lord is different, and deserves much deeper reflection than I am capable of here. The idea that our Lord, once conceived, could have been aborted, will surely be repugnant to many Christians. But there is the further point that Christians believe that in his Incarnation, our Lord was fully identifying himself with our humanity. Many Christians will therefore conclude that just as it is repugnant to think of aborting our Lord, so it ought to be repugnant to think of aborting any member of that human race with which our Lord has fully identified himself.

This brings us to the point where we must consider one of the most frequently-used biblical ideas, that of mankind being created in the image of God. We have already seen that the creation of man in the image of God forms the motive clause for the prohibition about shedding man's blood. However, what use can be made of the notion, as it appears in the Bible, for the abortion debate is not clear, certainly to me. Recent scholarly attempts to understand what was meant by the writer of Genesis 1:27 have been expressed in relational rather than ontological terms. The "image" has been taken to indicate man's stewardship over the world, as God's representative in it.[17] Or it has been interpreted as indicating man's unique ability within the created order to hear and respond to the voice of God.[18] Even if we assume that the "image" is asserting something ontological about mankind, what we do not know is whether the "image" (whatever it is) is present from the moment of conception, or whether, in Old Testament terms, it is there only after the "unformed substance" has reached its definite human form. In all honesty, I could not totally disregard the argument that accepted that the "image of God" in man was vital in the abortion debate, but which held that the "image" was not present before a certain point in the unborn child's development, and that abortions up to that point were in order. I do not agree with this point of view, but in fairness, I must say that nothing in the Bible clearly shows that the image of God is "present" from the moment of conception.

It is now time to turn from these largely negative observations. They have been deliberately presented because I think that the abortion issue is too important to be argued about in terms more suitable to a biblical and theological kindergarten. If the Bible can be used at all to support the pro-life position, it must be used in a manner calculated to gain the respect, if not the agreement, of intelligent people who desire more than literalist text-quoting. To this task we now address ourselves.

What follows is divided into three sections. The first section is about the Bible, based upon the view that the main purpose of the Bible is to express the witness to faith in God of the people of the Old and New Testaments, so that we might come to faith. The second section assumes that as well as being a "life" issue (in the sense defined), it is also a rights issue.

In Gerhard Ebeling's *The Nature of Faith* the following definition of the Bible is found:

> The Bible bears witness to a proclamation that has taken place and is the impulse for a proclamation which is to take place.[19]

This definition recognizes that the Bible was produced in specific historical and cultural circumstances, while allowing that the Bible is more than a guide to ancient history or ancient religion. It emphasizes that the Bible is a proclamation—in the Old Testament the proclamation that God is for his people; in the New Testament a proclamation that God is for all mankind in Jesus Christ. The main purpose of the Bible is to help us to respond to God who is the subject and the object of the proclamation. If we respond in faith, we shall find a new orientation for our lives, which we may wish to express in one or more of the biblical affirmations: "Jesus is Lord", "God has made him both Lord and Christ, this Jesus (who was) crucified", "If anyone is in Christ, there is a new creation".

To respond in faith to the proclamation contained in the Bible does not give access to information concerning the "nuts and bolts of life". A Christian does not possess superior knowledge about matters of medicine, science of morals, compared with non-Christians, but he finds himself confronted by the imperatives of the biblical proclamation about God: "You must love your neighbour as yourself."; "If anyone says 'I love God', and hates his brother, he is a liar."; "There is neither Jew nor Greek, there is neither slave nor free, there is neither male nor female, for you are all one in Christ Jesus."

Within the Bible itself, the effect of these imperatives upon social attitudes and actions can be clearly seen. In the version of the Ten Commandments in Deuteronomy 5:6-21, the exodus from Egypt is given as the reason why a man's servants and animals must be allowed to rest on the sabbath day. God had graciously delivered his people from bondage; they must graciously allow their servants to rest. The same motive clause is found in passages which command that provision should be made for the sojourner, the fatherless and the widow (Deuteronomy 24:19-22).

A most instructive passage is that relating to the release of slaves in Deuteronomy 15:12-18. If this is compared with Exodus 21:1-11, it will be seen immediately that Deuteronomy treats women slaves on an equal footing with male slaves, while Exodus 21 discriminates against women slaves. In fact the words "or a Hebrew woman" are clearly a later addition to Deuteronomy 15:12, as even the reader of an English version such as the R.S.V. can see (this is obscured in N.E.B. and G.N.B.) That the reference to the woman is a later addition is, however, most significant. It indicates a development within the biblical tradition, as a result of which the implications of God's having redeemed the Israelites from slavery in Egypt are extended to include women slaves as well as men slaves. In other words, the imperative based upon God's redeeming action is given a wider application.

This brings us to the heart of what I take to be proper use of the Bible in social and moral questions. It is to discover the imperatives which arise from the proclamation of God's redemption, and to apply those imperatives to the situations in which we find ourselves. In the parable of the Good Samaritan, Jesus did not define who was meant by "the neighbour". He left us a story that is quite frightening in the way in which it makes clear our responsibility to regard as our neighbour anyone, friend or foe, whom we perceive to be in need. It took Christian civilisation nearly 1,800 years to implement the full implications that there is neither slave nor free in Christ Jesus, and to abolish slavery.

This is not to say that the Bible is devoid of commandments and instructions laid upon Christians; far from it. The Ten Commandments, in their Old Testament formulation and in their New Testament distillation into love for God and for one's neighbour, still represent the core of the obedience to God of those who have come to faith in him. But it must never be forgotten that in using the Bible, Christians have traditionally been concerned with the spirit rather than the letter, and have not hesitated to pick and choose what they held to be binding upon them. In Acts 15, the apostolic Church required only four things of Gentiles who had become Christians : abstention from food offered to idols, from fornication, from meat not ritually killed, and from eating blood. The demand that they should be required to observe the Mosaic law was rejected.[20] Again, in the 39 articles, only those laws of the Old Testament deemed to be moral (as opposed to Old Testament civil laws or laws concerned with rites and ceremonies) are held to be binding upon Christians.[21]

The way forward in using the Bible in the abortion debate seems to involve exploring the demands of the biblical imperatives of salvation, rather than in searching for texts that can be literally applied in the debate.

This brings us to the second section, which concerns us with the sense in which we should regard abortion as a "life" issue. The two main definitions of "life" that are relevant are life understood in biological terms, and life understood in relational terms. The first definition is implied in the charge sometimes made against pro-life supporters, that they ought to have the same concern for the animals whose meat they consume, as for the unborn children whose lives they seek to protect. While there is much to be said to support vegetarianism, including the fact that it enables us to respect the rights of animals, it has to be emphasized that what pro-life supporters are mainly concerned to protect are potential human beings whose destiny it is not merely to exist biologically, but to share human relationships, and to love and to be loved. In this connection, the imperative of salvation that "life depends upon love" becomes important.

At the heart of the Christian proclamation is the belief that it is the love of God which makes possible the Christian life. Perhaps the passage that comes nearest to saying this explicitly is Galatians 2:20: '... the life I now live in the flesh I live by faith in the Son of God, who loved me and gave himself for me.' But the notion is implicit in many parts of the Bible. The life which Israel enjoyed in the presence of God was made possible only by his love, even if that love was repeatedly cast back into his face: 'When Israel was a child, I loved him, and out of Egypt I called my son' (Hosea 11:1). In the New Testament, it was the fact that the Good Samaritan in the parable was "moved with compassion" that saved from certain death the man who had been robbed and beaten. In the parable of the Prodigal Son it was the love of the father that made possible the renewed life of the son who had been "dead, and is alive again" (Luke 15:24). The very possibility of Christian life depends on the fact that God commends his love towards us "in that while we were yet sinners Christ died for us" (Romans 5:8).

The link between life and love is also apparent in non-religious contexts. Loneliness and isolation are not things that can be easily borne. Often, even the affection of a cat or a dog can help to enrich the life of a lonely person. The relationships that may develop between a kidnapped hostage and his kidnappers may be the best hope for the saving of his life. The more that people respond to each other as persons, the less easy it becomes to think of killing. In the case of handicapped children, the love of those who care for them can enrich their lives; and the response of the handicapped is itself ennobling to others.

If it is true that life depends upon love, it also seems to be true that disregard for life militates against love. It takes hardness and callousness to carry through the sort of destruction of human life that this century has perfected. It is rumoured that first World War generals who were sensitive about the level of casualties among their men were distrusted by the General Staff. In order to carry out mass killings, it is often necessary to present the intended victims as less than human. Jews become "vermin", and brave soldiers on the other side become the "enemy" whose lives are as expendable as those of our own side are meant to be precious.

If, at the heart of the gospel, it is the love of God which makes life in a relational sense possible, the Christian is called to resist any degradation of the life of any human being, friend or foe, who is potentially a son or daughter of God, and thus a sister or brother.

In the case of unborn children, it now seems to be clear that from the moment of fertilization, that "programming" is present in the fertilized ovum which makes it unique, and which determines the physical and mental characteristics that will continue the best hope for the saving of his life. The more that people adolescent stages to full maturity. Can we, at one and the same time, be under the imperative of love, and be satisfied with a society that denies to the unborn the possibility of living? What sort of a society is it that leaves it to small voluntary agencies to try to persuade mothers who are bearing "unwanted" children to let those children live, while there are many families in which love will make a full life possible for "unwanted" and "rejected" children? It is no part of this essay to adopt a superior moral attitude towards mothers who find themselves bearing unwanted children. What a Christian society ought to do, however, is to stress that the love of God stretching out to the unwanted and the unworthy is at the heart of the gospel, and that the practical application of this imperative in all its ramifications is a task laid upon the Church.

This leads us to the third section, which is about rights. One of the paradoxes of the present century is that, on the one hand, it has seen more brutal destruction of human lives than in any previous century; but second, it has seen a remarkable growth of sensitivity to the rights of minorities and the defenceless. The Bible has much to say about minorities and the defenceless, under the imperative that "the strong must defend the weak".

There are many passages, especially in the Old Testament, where this imperative is asserted explicitly. Of the ideal king in Psalm 72 it is prayed:

> May he defend the cause of the poor of the people,
> give deliverance to the needy, and crush the oppressor!

The shepherds (i.e. the rulers) in Ezekiel 34 are condemned because they have not cared for the weak.

> The weak you have not strengthened, the sick you have not
> bound up, the strayed you have not brought back, the lost
> you have not sought ... (v.4)

In Psalm 82, God appears to condemn the divine beings whom
he had set over the foreign nations, to see that justice prevailed
among them:

> How long will you judge unjustly and show partiality to the
> wicked?
> Give justice to the weak and the fatherless;
> maintain the right of the afflicted and the destitute.
> Rescue the weak and the needy;
> deliver them from the hand of the wicked (vv. 2-4).

In applying this imperative to our present world, we must include
the unborn among the weak and defenceless. They cannot speak
for themselves, and because they cannot be seen in everyday life,
their uniqueness as individuals is overlooked. They are as much
in need of defence as are people who are wrongly imprisoned and
are as easily eradicated from our consciences.

The main burden of this essay is that the use of the Bible is not
a matter of selecting texts and of trying to apply them as though
they were legislation for modern situations. The point that has
been stressed is that the Bible's primary function is to bring us to
faith and to keep us in faith. The faith which we confess is faith
in a God who responds to human heed, who justifies the un-
righteous and who seeks the outcast. The Bible lays upon us
imperatives that derive from the heart of our salvation, and our
task is to work out those imperatives in the situation in which we
find ourselves.

Abortion has always been a feature within human society.
Probably for much of human history, it was practised on a small
scale and was based upon ignorance of the precise medical and
scientific facts of the beginnings of life.[22] Today, we know that
from the earliest moments of life, a unique individual is present
in the womb. But also today, we have become tolerant of the destruction and cheapening of human lives in many ways (including
plans for future so-called nuclear defence) and we have developed
techniques for the relatively safe and convenient termination of
pregnancies on a large scale. The Bible does not address itself

directly to this latter problem. What it does is to challenge us to include unborn children along with the defenceless and minorities whose task it is for the strong to defend. What it does is to ask us whether at one and the same time we can assert our faith in a God who seeks the unworthy and the unwanted, and be indifferent to the fact that thousands of unwanted unborn children have their individuality terminated. The Bible does not provide us with "knock down" arguments that take from us the responsibility of being informed and of entering into dialogue with those who find abortion unobjectionable. The debate about abortion is a debate about an issue which demands of Christians that they think deeply about what the heart of Christian faith is, and how that faith is to be expressed in a world that appears to know little of the true spirit of Jesus Christ.

Abortion footnotes

1. Genesis 4:1 and some 30 other occurrences in a non-metaphorical sense.
2. cp. 2 Samuel 11:4-5.
3. *The Translator's New Testament*, London 1973, p.2.
4. S. Krauss, *Talmudische Archälogie*, Vol. II, Leipzig 1911 (reprint Hildesheim 1966), pp.3 ff. and p.424 notes 1 ff.
5. *Ibid.*
6. The Hebrew word *golem* which occurs in the Bible only at Psalm 139:16, but which is attested in post-biblical Hebrew means "a rolled up, shapeless mass, whence 1) lump, a shapeless or lifeless substance" according to M. Jastrow, *A Dictionary of the Targumim, the Talmud Babli and Yerushalmi, and the Midrashic Literature,* reprint New York 1950, Vol. I p. 222.
7. Job 3:16. The word rendered "untimely birth" is related to the verb "to fall".
8. See the article by J.S. Licht, Ledah (giving birth) in *Encyclopaedia Biblica* IV, Jerusalem 1962, pp.431-435 (Hebrew).
9. See Licht, *loc. cit.* The information, in Genesis 50:23, that Joseph's sons were born upon his knees may denote that the father assisted with the birth, or that after the birth he took them onto his knees as a sign of welcoming into the family.
10. See T.J. Meek, "The Middle Assyrian Laws" in J.B. Pritchard, *Ancient Near Eastern Tests relating to the Old Testament.* Princeton 1955[2], p.185. G.R. Driver and J.C. Miles *The Babylonian Laws*, Vol. I Oxford 1952, p.367 assume that abortion was practised in Babylon as well as Assyria.
11. Psalm 127:4, "Like arrows in the hand of a warrior are the sons of one's youth".

12. See Numbers 5:11-31.
13. See S. Loewenstamm, *Mamzer* in *Encyclopaedia Biblica*, Vol. V, Jerusalem 1968, pp.2-3. If *mamzer* does not mean the offspring of an incestuous union, it may denote a child of a mixed marriage. For the death penalty for incest see Leviticus 18:6 ff.
14. See J. Weingreen, "The Concepts of Retaliation and Compensation in Biblical Law", *Proceedings of the Royal Irish Academy*, Vol. 76, Section C, No. 1, 1976, pp.1-11.
15. Thus, *Abortion. A Matter of Life and Death*, Belfast 1981, section one, para. B.
16. cp. St. Luke 13:16.
17. See H.W. Wolff, *Anthropology of the Old Testament*, London 1974, pp.159 ff.
18. See the important Excursus on Genesis 1:26-7 in C. Westermann, *Genesis (Biblischer Kommentar)* 1,3, Neukirchen Vluyn 1968, pp.203-214.
19. G. Ebeling, *The Nature of Faith*, London (Fontana) 1966, p.103.
20. Acts 15, esp. vv. 5, 20, 28-9.
21. Article VII "Of the Old Testament".
22. For ancient knowledge of the medical facts see the articles "Abtreibung" and "Embryologie" in *Reallexikon für die Antike und Christentum*, Stuttgart 1950 ff.

5

Abortion and Early Christian Thought[1]

G. BONNER

In his *Apology* (A.D. 197) the early Christian writer Tertullian, dealing with the common pagan allegation that Christians sacrificed infants in their religious rites, retorted with characteristic, bitter irony, that the pagans were merely assigning their own practices to the Christians who were, by the very nature of their religious profession, forbidden to do anything of the kind.

> As regards infanticide, however—although I grant that murder of a child, if it is your own, differs from killing somebody else!—it makes no difference whether it is done wilfully or as part of a sacred rite. I will turn to you now as a nation. How many of the crowd standing round us, open-mouthed for Christian blood, how many of you, gentlemen, magistrates most just and strict against us, shall I not prick in your own inner consciousness as being the slayers of your own offspring? There is, indeed, a difference in the manner of death; but assuredly it is more cruel to drown an infant or expose it to cold and starvation and the dogs (than to sacrifice it, as you allege that we do)—even an adult would prefer to die by the sword. But for us, to whom homicide has been once for all forbidden, it is not permitted to break up even

what has been conceived in the womb, while the blood is still being drawn from the mother's body to make a new creature. Prevention of birth is premature murder, and it makes no difference whether it is a life already born that one snatches away or a life that is coming to birth that one destroys. The future man is a man already: the whole fruit is present in the seed.[2]

Tertullian's assertion that abortion was forbidden to Christians represents the universal teaching of the early Church. Any appeal to Christian antiquity as a guide to moral conduct in the present age will, on this particular issue, receive only one answer. It is not, however, enough simply to appeal to antiquity; for while fundamental principles of morality remain constant, their application at any particular time is conditioned by circumstances which are capable of being altered by new factors. A familiar example in the late twentieth century is the problem which arises from the ability of medical science to extend a human life, which, in an earlier century, would certainly have perished, in a kind of vegetative existence, of little apparent value to the patient concerned. For similar reasons it is possible that, under modern conditions, the practice of abortion may, on occasion, have a justification which could not have been urged in classical antiquity.

There is, moreover, a further consideration. Abortion, in the Graeco-Roman world, was neither the only nor necessarily the most common method of disposing of unwanted offspring. Indeed, as Tertullian observes in the passage quoted above, infanticide, usually by the practice of exposure, was generally accepted and eventually banned only under the influence of Christianity. The notion that a child, once born, was a human being enjoying the same right to life as an adult, was very far from being generally accepted. On the contrary, the survival of the child during the first few days following the birth depended to a great degree upon the decision of the father who thus retained, in an attenuated form, something of the power of life and death enjoyed by the head of the family in early Roman society. This residual patriarchal power perished with the triumph of Christianity; but the notion that parents had a right ver the fate of the newly-born survived, to be canvassed afresh in our own day, at least in the case of children born deformed or mentally deficient, in the interest (it is urged) of parents and child alike, and with the approval of an influential section of the medical profession. Thus questions debated in the first Christian centuries remain relevant in the twentieth, and if we seek to draw practical conclusions from them, we need to know the circumstances and the terms in which they were discussed. History may not repeat itself, but moral questions seem to have a tendency to recur.

'Children', declared the psalmist, 'and the fruit of the womb are an heritage and gift that cometh of the Lord.' Such sentiments are generally echoed in pre-industrial societies. Quite apart from the natural pleasure afforded by children, a numerous progeny provides physical assistance in communities devoid of all but the most primitive tools and appliances, and an insurance against physical destitution and neglect in old age. Childlessness is both a misfortune and a reproach; the birth of sons is to be eagerly awaited and welcomed. 'Happy is the man that hath his quiver full of them. They shall not be ashamed when they speak with their enemies in the gate.'

Yet children are not an unmixed blessing in primitive society. Increase of population, however desirable, must be set against the resources available to feed it. Too many mouths bring famine, and famine brings death. In such circumstances, it may seem best to anticipate the inevitable and decline to rear a child who seems destined to become a useless mouth and a burden to society as a whole. This can be done by abortion, but there are many objections to abortion in primitive societies; it may well be dangerous, and bring about the death of the mother as well as of her offspring;[3] but besides this, it is an indiscriminate method of population control, which carries off the desirable, as well as the unwanted, child. This applies particularly in the case of sex, for a son may be welcomed when a girl is discarded. In such circumstances it may be deemed best to allow the mother to give birth and then decide whether or not the infant is to be permitted to live. In the Graeco-Roman world, if the decision were hostile, the solution was either to kill or, not uncommonly, to expose the unwanted infant, a procedure which spared the parents from directly shedding blood, and gave the child the possibility—albeit a slim one—of survival, if some rich and childless woman were

looking for an adopted heir.[4] The fortunes of such lucky sur-
vivors (a small minority) provided a theme for Greek drama.

Modern historians are more inclined to dwell upon the fate of
the majority. 'It is strange and horrible to think', writes one,
'that any day on your walks abroad in a Greek city you might
come across a "pot-exposed" infant, as the Athenians call them,
in a corner of the market-place or by a wrestling-ground, at the
entrance of a temple or in a consecrated cave, and that you might
see a slave-girl timidly peeping round to look if the child might
yet be saved, or running back to bear the news to the broken-
hearted young mother.'[5] 'Until the beginning of the third-
century [A.D.], when abandoning a child was considered the
equivalent of murder,' writes another, '[a Roman father] might
expose his new-born child to perish of cold and hunger or to be
devoured by dogs on one of the public refuse dumps, unless it
was rescued by the pity of some passer-by.'[6] Christians, of
course, denounced the practice. The anonymous author of the
Epistle to Diognetus (second century?) finds it necessary to make
it clear that, while Christians marry like other folk and have
children, 'they do not expose their offspring'[7] and we have
already seen Tertullian's sarcastic reference to exposure.

Exposure was a barbarous, but generally accepted, custom in
the Graeco-Roman world; the geographer Strabo (c.64 B.C.–
A.D.19) thought it worthy to record that the Egyptians—like the
Jews—reared all their children;[8] but it proceeded from economic
pressures rather than from mere hardness of heart. One of the
most pathetic letters which has come down to us from antiquity
was written in 1 B.C. by a man named Hilarion, working in
Alexandria, to his wife, Alis: 'I beg and beseech you to take care
of the little child, and as soon as we receive wages I will send
them to you. If ... you bear offspring, if it is a male, let it live; if it
is a female, expose it.'[9] It is not necessary to ascribe particular
heartlessness to the writer,[10] who could consign a daughter to
death while preserving a son. He did no more than follow con-
vention in a male-dominated society in which a superfluity of
females was an economic liability. 'Everyone, even if poor, rears
a son,' wrote a Greek comic writer, 'but even a rich man exposes
a daughter.'[11] There might, however, be other and more tragic
motives than financial necessity. A slave woman might shrink
from the burden of raising children in her servile condition, and

either procure an abortion or make away with the infant after birth.[12]

Infanticide, a term which would include exposure, was made a capital offence by a law of the Christian emperors Valentinian I, Valens and Gratian of 7 February 374.[13] It would appear, from the evidence of the Roman jurist Paulus, that this principle was already established in the reign of Severus Alexander (222-235), an emperor traditionally credited with sympathy towards Christianity.[14] Tertullian, writing in 197, asserts that legislation against infanticide already existed in his day, but claims that it was a dead letter;[15] and what he says is borne out by the paucity of any pagan protest against infanticide. The aristocratic Roman philosopher Seneca the Younger (*c.*4 B.C.—A.D.65), for example, remarks complacently that 'unnatural progeny (*fetus*) we destroy; we drown even children, who at birth are weakly and abnormal,'[16] and even when a Stoic like Caius Musonius Rufus (*c.*20—*c.*90) was moved to protest against the killing or exposure of infants, he appeals, not to the rights of the child, but to the dignity and utility afforded by a large family.[17]

Nevertheless, despite the relative indifference of the majority of pagans to the moral issues of infanticide, there is evidence of a distaste felt by some of the more sensitive, which led them to commend abortion as an alternative. Plato, in the ideal state described in his *Republic*,[18] laid it down as a matter of eugenic policy that parents should bear children for the state for a defined period of years. After that period sexual intercourse would still be permitted, but the couple involved should make every effort to prevent any children conceived from seeing the light (by abortion) and dispose of the new-born child (by infanticide) only if the former course proved impossible. Similarly Aristotle, although holding the common Greek view that deformed children ought not to be reared, objected to the exposure of healthy infants merely as a method of population control. In his view the size of the family should be determined by the state, and if children were conceived in excess of the permitted number, an abortion should be procured at an early stage of pregnancy, 'before sensation and life develop in the embryo'.[19] This process of formation or animation, manifested by the movement of the fetus in the womb, took place, in Aristotle's opinion, on the fortieth day of pregnancy in the case of a male child and on the

ninetieth of a female, and abortion would be justified or condemned by the presence or absence of sensation and life.[20] This
view of fetal development, with its distinction between the
formed fetus, which is in effect a human being, and the
unformed fetus, which is not, was accepted, for reasons which
will hereafter appear, by one school of Christian thought in the
later Roman Empire as justifying abortion at an early stage of
pregnancy; but the opinion of the majority of the Fathers was
utterly against any such distinction, and we find St Basil the
Great, writing in 374, declaring roundly that abortion was
murder, and that no distinction between the formed and the
unformed fetus was admissible in Christian morality.[21]

The Aristotelian view of fetal development was not, however,
the only one which prevailed in the ancient world. The Stoics,
who were perhaps the most important philosophical influence on
the Roman mind, held that the fetus was no more than a part of
the mother's body during the entire duration of pregnancy and
was ensouled only at birth by a species of cooling by the air,
which transformed a mere lump of flesh into a living and sentient
being.[22] On such a view, of course, any question of the morality
of abortion becomes irrelevant, except in terms of an operation
necessary for the health of the mother or the well-being of the
family. It was for this reason that a Stoic like Musonius Rufus,
who disapproved of abortion, was forced to address his arguments to paternal self-interest and family pride, for the fetus
itself could have no rights, since as a human being it was non-
existent.[23]

This philosophical view of the non-humanity of the child in
the womb was endorsed by the Roman jurists. According to
Papinian (d.212) what is unborn cannot rightly be called a man;[24]
while Ulpian (d.228) maintains that the fetus, before it is born, is
a part of a woman or of her viscera.[25] The unborn child is not yet
a participant in human affairs. Given such opinions on the part
of the lawyers it is hardly surprising that abortion, when it was
condemned, was condemned as an offence against the parent, not
the child. Cicero spoke with approval of the case of an Asian
woman who was sentenced to death for having aborted herself in
return for a bribe offered by the reversionary heirs of her
husband's estate, whose expectations would have been disappointed if she had borne a child. Cicero approved of the

sentence, not because the offender had destroyed her child but—significantly—because she had disappointed the hope of her husband for offspring, erased the memory of his name, prevented the replenishment of the race and the chance of a family heir, and deprived the state of a citizen.[26] Similarly, in the reigns of the Emperors Septimius Severus and Caracallus (198—208) a law was issued punishing with exile a woman who aborted herself, 'for it would seem indecent for her to have cheated her husband of children with impunity'.[27] Here again it is not the child but the father whose interests are considered.

Nevertheless, despite the philosophical and judicial indifference to the ethical issues raised by abortion, there were some pagans like Musonius Rufus who disapproved of it. The Hippocratic Oath, (see pp.29f above) so influential in the history of Greek medicine (and medicine continued to be very much a Greek science in the Roman world, expressly prohibited the physician from procuring an abortion,[28] though in practice physicians were prepared to perform an embryotomy or a craniotomy where a child could not be delivered, acting with what the Christian Tertullian calls a 'necessary cruelty'.[29] Again, the Stoic philosopher, who had spoken of infanticide with such detachment, found it a matter for praise in his mother, Helvia, that, unlike many of her contemporaries, she had never had recourse to abortion.[30] More surprising is the protest of Ovid, the butterfly-poet of the Augustan age, whose elegant eroticism, once deemed scandalous enough to be used as an excuse for sending the author into exile, now seems very modest in comparison with contemporary pornography. In two of his poems Ovid refers to his mistress, Corinna (whether she was a real woman or a literary invention cannot be decided and is irrelevant for our purposes) who, in order to avoid the disfigurement of post-puerperal stretch-marks, had deliberately aborted herself and come dangerously near to death as a consequence. From his verses it would appear that Ovid, of whom it has been said that 'although easily moved he was not a man of deep feeling',[31] sincerely disapproved of Corinna's action. Revealingly, he addresses his first poem to Isis, the loving mother-goddess of Egypt, the land where all children are reared, and implores her to pardon the fault, and so spare two lives: Corinna's, and that of her lover, Ovid.[32] To Corinna herself Ovid addresses arguments which are in no way less persuasive for being obvious. What would have happened to the human race if earlier generations had practised abortion? What indeed would have been the fate of Corinna, if her own mother had decided to make away with her?[33] Ovid concludes his second poem with a prayer to the kindly gods to pardon one sin in his beloved (*pecasse semel concedite tuto*) and to punish only a second offence.

Ovid's denunciation of abortion is effective as far as it goes, but it does not go very far. He has a kindly feeling for the unborn child and regrets its destruction; but his concern is based as much upon the insult offered to the gods by Corinna's action as by the hurt to the aborted fetus. At heart it is the consequences of the sin for the sinner, and not the sin itself, which concern Ovid, for Corinna's action would have been treated lightly in the social world in which she moved, and could hardly have been deemed criminal by the prevailing attitude in the Roman world towards the fetus, namely, that it was no more than a part of its mother.

There was, however, at the beginning of the Christian era another view of the nature of the fetus which stood in stark opposition to the prevailing opinions of Graeco-Roman society. It may be called the Judaeo-Platonic view, with the emphasis upon the Jewish element. This was the attitude which the Christian Church inherited, and which may be said to have prevailed among the majority of Christian moral theologians to the present day. It would, however, be ungrateful in a Christian not to recognize the fact that it was in Jewish circles that the view first found expression.

Put briefly, the Judaeo-Platonic view regards the fetus as a living being endowed with a soul either from the moment of its conception or during the pregnancy. In part, this view derives from the Platonic belief that man is essentially a soul making use of a body. Plato, and some of his school, were prepared to entertain a theory of transmigration of souls from one body to another; but such a notion was naturally unacceptable to Jews and Christians. For them the soul and body had to constitute one humanity, and it came easily to them to conceive of that unity as being effected at the time of conception.

Here, the teaching of an unknown Christian elder, quoted by Clement of Alexandria (who died before 215), is particularly interesting. For him the fetus in the womb is a living being (*zoön*). The soul is introduced into the womb by an angel (the elder has in mind the angelic visitation of Luke 1:13 in this context) and associates itself with the vivifying principle (*pneuma*), which is in the male seed, to fashion the embryo from the blood of the mother.[34] On such a view the fetus must be judged human from the moment of conception, and the elder points to the case of John the Baptist leaping in his mother's womb (Luke 1:41) as evidence for his contention.

However, before the teaching of the anonymous Christian elder cited by Clement, a somewhat similar position had been reached by the Jewish Platonist, Philo of Alexandria, based upon the authority of the Greek version of the Old Testament. In Exodus 21:22,23 the Hebrew text runs:

> And if men strive together, and hurt a woman with child, so that her fruit depart, and yet no mischief follow [i.e. to the woman]: he shall surely be fined, according as the woman's husband shall lay upon him; and he shall pay as the judge determine. But if any mischief follow, then thou shalt give life for life (Revised Version).

The thought behind these injunctions is very much that of the legislation of the ancient Near East.[35] The fetus is not regarded as human, and its destruction may be atoned for by a fine. 'But if any mischief follow'—that is, if the pregnant woman dies as a result of her injury—then the offence is deemed to be murder, and demands the death penalty. (See also page 81.)

When, however, the Greek translation of the Old Testament known as the Septuagint came to be made, in Egypt and probably before the middle of the third century B.C. for the use of a Jewish community ignorant of Hebrew, the wording of Exodus 21:22,23 underwent a decisive change:

> And if two men strive and smite a woman with child, and her child be born imperfectly formed, he shall be forced to pay a penalty: as the woman's husband shall lay upon him he shall pay with a valuation. But if it be perfectly formed, he shall give life for life.

In this version the formed fetus was to be accorded full human status, and its destruction regarded as equivalent to murder. It is not clear how this textual transformation came into the Septuagint. The distinction between the formed and the unformed fetus suggests the influence of Greek medical theory and implies that the alteration was the work of the translators, rather than being derived from some Hebrew version other than the standard Masoretic text; but the question is, for our purposes, academic. The important fact is that the Jews of Alexandria used a text of Exodus 21:22,23 in which the fetus, if formed, was regarded as a human being.

This principle governs the teaching of Philo (born *c*. 25 B.C. and died before A.D.50), the Jewish philosopher of Alexandria. A devoutly observant Jew, Philo was also a product of Greek culture. Nevertheless, he remained first and foremost a Jew for whom the Bible, in the Greek Septuagint translation which he believed to be of divine inspiration, was the supreme and infallible guide on all matters of belief and conduct. Thus, in the case of abortion, Philo holds that if the fetus is unshaped and undeveloped, the man responsible must be punished with a fine, 'but if the offspring is already shaped and all the limbs have their proper qualities and places in the system, he must die, for that which answers to this description is a human being, which he has destroyed in the workshop of Nature, who judges that the hour has not yet come for bringing it out into the light, like a statue lying in a studio, requiring nothing more than to be conveyed outside and released from confinement.'[36] Philo is aware of the Stoic theory that the child remains part of its mother until birth, but for him the divine Law must take precedence over medical theory[37] It goes without saying that if he rejects abortion, Philo is even more vehemently opposed to infanticide, and denounces those who destroy or expose their children in the strongest terms.[38] Except for his distinction between the formed and the unformed fetus—a distinction forced upon him by the version of Scripture which he used—Philo's attitude to abortion and infanticide anticipates that of the most rigorous of the later Fathers of the Christian Church.

It might be suggested that Philo, a native of Alexandria who may well not have known Hebrew, is not necessarily representative of the beliefs of Palestinian Jewry. In this matter we are, however, able to confirm his teaching by the evidence of a Palestinian Jew, Joseph ben Matthias, better known as Flavius

Josephus (37—*c*.100), who, although a deserter to the Romans during the Jewish War (66—73), remained loyal to his religion. In his work against the antisemitic writer Apion, Josephus declares: '[The Law] orders all the offspring to be brought up and forbids women either to cause abortion or to make away with the fetus; a woman convicted of this is regarded as an infanticide, because she destroys a soul and diminishes the race.'[39] The scope of Josephus' remarks is rather different from that of Philo. Philo is concerned primarily with the exegesis of a text of Scripture; Josephus, it would seem, with its practical application in everyday life. Thus he refers specifically to a woman who procures an abortion, whether upon herself or upon another, as midwives might on occasion be tempted to do.[40] The principle, however, remains unaltered; and opposition to abortion, except in the rarest circumstances, remains part of Jewish ethics to the present day.[41]

With this Jewish heritage, it is not surprising that Christianity from the first denounced abortion no less than infanticide. The *Didache* or *Teaching of the Twelve Apostles*, a manual of Church order and discipline, probably to be dated not later than A.D.100 and possibly as early as A.D.60 declares: 'Thou shalt not procure abortion or commit infanticide,'[42] linking these practices to the sins of murder, adultery, sodomy, fornication, theft, sorcery and covetousness. In a similar fashion the so-called *Epistle of Barnabas*, a pseudonymous production from Alexandrian circles, concerned to warn Christians against a Judaistic understanding of the Old Testament, and probably to be assigned to the end of the first century A.D. or the beginning of the second, echoes the *Didache*: 'Thou shalt not procure abortion, thou shalt not commit infanticide.'[43] Again, Athenagoras, the Christian apologist, whose *Supplication for the Christians* is addressed to the Emperors Marcus Aurelius and Commodus, and therefore can be dated between 176 and 180, not only rejects abortion and infanticide but makes it clear that the fetus is to be regarded as a living being while in its mother's womb. Replying to the common pagan allegation that the Christians sacrificed infants in their rituals, he writes:

> . . . what sense does it make to think of us as murderers
> when we say that women who practise abortion are mur-
> derers and will render account to God for abortion? The

same man cannot regard that which is in the womb as a living being (*zoön*) and for that reason an object of God's concern and then murder it when it has come into the light. Neither can the same man forbid exposing a child that has been born on the grounds that those who do so are murderers and then slay one that has been nourished. On the contrary, we remain the same and unchanging in every way and at all times: we are servants of reason and not its masters.[44]

Clement of Alexandria, whose lifespan would seem to have been approximately contemporary with that of Athenagoras, takes a similar view. Our life will be lived according to nature if from the very beginning of marriage we restrain our desires and do not destroy the race of men, which is born by divine providence, by wicked and malicious devices, 'for women who, in order to conceal fornication, make use of deadly medicines which lead directly to ruin, destroy all humanity along with the fetus.'[45]

Such denunciation of abortion and infanticide expressed by handbooks of Church discipline like the *Didache* and in the writings of educated Christians like Athenagoras and Clement is echoed in the popular literature of the early Church. *The Apocalypse of Peter*, one of those apocryphal scriptures which had so great a vogue in the early Christian centuries, is to be dated around A.D.135. Originally composed in Greek, of which only fragments remain, it survives today in an Ethiopic translation. *The Apocalypse of Peter* provides one of those visions of Heaven and Hell which were eventually to find their fullest and most majestic expression in Dante's *Divine Comedy*. In a terrible and lurid picture the *Apocalypse* describes the punishment of those who have procured abortions and exposed children:

> . . . And near this flame there is a great and very deep pit and into it there flow all kinds of things from everywhere: judgement (?), horrifying things and excretions. And the women [are] swallowed up [by this] up to their necks and are punished with great pain. These are they who have procured abortions and have ruined the work of God which He has created. Opposite them is another place where the children sit, but both alive, and they cry to God. And lightnings go forth from those children which pierce the eyes of

those who, by fornication, have brought about their destruction. Other men and women stand above them naked.
And their children stand opposite to them in a place of
delight. And they sigh and cry to God because of their
parents: 'These are they who neglected and cursed and
transgressed Thy commandment. They killed us and cursed
the angel who created [us] and hung us up. And they
withheld from us the light which Thou hast appointed for
all.' And the milk of the mothers flows from their breasts
and congeals and smells foul, and from it come forth beasts
that devour flesh, which turn and torture them for ever with
their husbands, because they forsook the commandment of
God and killed their children. And the children shall be
given to the angel Tempakos. And those who slew them
will be tortured for ever, for God wills it to be so.[46]

This description of the punishment of abortionists is repeated
in the later *Apocalypse of Paul*, which was certainly known to St.
Augustine of Hippo in the early fifth century, and which may
have been known to Origen in the third. As in *The Apocalypse of
Peter*, the narrator of *The Apocalypse of Paul* provides a lurid description of the other world and of the joys and torments which
await men there:

. . . I asked and said: Who are these men and women who
are strangled in the fire and pay the penalty? And he
answered me: They are the women who defiled what God
has fashioned (*commaculantes plasma Dei*), bringing forth
children from the womb (*proferentes ex utero infantes*) and
they are the men who went to bed with them. However,
their children appealed to the Lord God and the angels who
are [set] over the punishments, saying: 'Defend us from our
parents, for they have defiled what is fashioned by God;
they have the name of God but they do not keep His commandments, and they gave us to be food for dogs and to be
trampled by pigs, and they threw others into the river.' But
those children were handed over to the angels of Tartarus,
who were over the punishments, that they should lead them
into a spacious place of mercy. However their fathers and
mothers were strangled in an everlasting punishment.[47]

The language of this passage is ambiguous; it is not wholly
clear whether it refers simply to infanticide, or to abortion as

well. The sentence, 'They gave us to be food for dogs and to be trampled by pigs, and they threw others into the river', reads like a description of infanticide—we remember Seneca: 'We drown even children, who at birth are weakly or deformed' and Tertullian: 'Assuredly it is more cruel to drown an infant or expose it to cold and starvation and the dogs [than to sacrifice it].' However, the sentence, 'They are the women who defiled what God has fashioned', suggests abortion, with the Latin phrase *commaculantes plasma Dei* corresponding to the Greek *phthoreis plasmatos Theou*—'corrupters of God's creation'— found in the *Didache* (5.2).

Finally, in the Christian Sibyllines, those curious fabrications of Jewish origin, ascribed to the pagan prophetesses called Sibyls and composed in the second century A.D., we find an un-equivocal condemnation of abortion in the most savage terms:

> . . . those who defiled their flesh with lewdness,
> And all who loosed the maiden girdle
> In stealthy union, and women who slay the burden
> Of the womb, and all who lawlessly cast out their offspring;
> Wizards and witches with them, them also
> The wrath of the heavenly and incorruptible God
> Shall bring to the pillory, where in circle all about
> Flows unwearied the fiery stream, and all of them together
> The angels of the immortal, everlasting God
> Shall punish fearfully with flaming whips,
> Binding them tightly about with fiery chains
> And unbreakable fetters; then in the dead of night
> Shall they be flung into Gehenna among the beasts of
>   Tartarus,
> Many and fearful, where darkness has no measure.[48]

The apocryphal Apocalypses and the Christian Sibylline Oracles indicate that denunciation of abortion was not confined to the higher levels of Christian life and practice, but was an integral part of the popular Christian moral code.

Among Christian theologians who denounced abortion, Tertullian occupies a highly important, if not decisive place, since he unequivocally equates abortion with murder. 'Prevention of birth', he declares, 'is premature murder, and it makes no dif-ference whether it is a life already born that one snatches away or a life that is coming to birth.'[49] As a matter of physiology, Tertullian believes that both body and soul are conceived and formed simultaneously;[50] and although he accepts the teaching of the Septuagint version of Exodus 21:22,23, with its distinction between the formed and the unformed fetus:—'The embryo . . . becomes a human being in the womb from the moment that its form is completed'[51]—he does not in practice make any such distinction. 'The future man is a man already: the whole fruit is present in the seed.'

Tertullian's contemporary, the African lawyer Minucius Felix, takes a similar line. 'Among you', he makes his Christian friend, Octavius, say to the pagans, 'I see newly-born sons at times exposed to wild beasts and birds, or violently strangled to a painful death; and there are women who, by medicinal draughts, extinguish in the womb and commit infanticide upon the offspring yet unborn. Such practices of course follow the precedents set by your gods; Saturn did not indeed expose his sons but devoured them.'[52] The word used by Minucius Felix here translated 'infanticide' is *parricidium*, the murder of a parent or other close relative, a crime which aroused a particular horror among the Romans, as it does in most human society. The word occurs again in a letter of St Cyprian, bishop of Carthage from 248/9 to 258, in which Cyprian refers to the presbyter Novatus, a sower of ecclesiastical discord, who is said to have aborted his wife by a kick administered during pregnancy, 'by which the son who was going to be born was killed'.[53]

The prohibition of abortion early passed into the law of the Church. Originally, it would seem, it was punished by a lifelong exclusion from communion, and the sacrament was not even administered on the penitent's death-bed; but in 314 the Council of Ancyra (the modern Turkish capital, Ankara) decreed as a concession that the period of penance should be reduced to ten years.[54] This canon (21) of the Council of Ancyra was destined to exercise a notable influence on the subsequent history of ecclesiastical discipline. St Basil the Great, in a letter written in 374, while rejecting any distinction between the formed or the unformed fetus, and adding to its destruction by abortion the further crime, that the woman involved endangered her own life, nevertheless accepted the term of ten years' penance laid down at Ancyra, and added that the period should be determined, not by time but by the character of repentance.[55] In the West the twenty-first canon of Ancyra was incorporated by the famous canonist Ivo of Chartres (c.1040-1115) into his *Decretum*[56] from whence it passed into the *Penitential* of Bartholomew, bishop of Exeter from 1167 to 1184.[57] Bartholomew also incorporated a canon—the canon *Si Aliquis*, destined to exercise an important influence on subsequent Church law—ascribed to a Council of Worms[58] by Burchard of Worms in his *Decretum*, written between 1007 and 1015,[59] though really by Regino of Prüm (c.840-915),[60] which equated the destruction of what had been conceived with murder.[61] Burchard also added a provision from a Roman source, imposing a three-year penance on all women who voluntarily procured an abortion.[62]

In tracing the development of the prohibition of abortion in medieval canon law we have, for the moment, passed over the teaching of the later Christian Fathers of the fourth and fifth centuries. These, no less than their predecessors, were inflexibly opposed to abortion, though many of them admitted a distinction of guilt based upon Exodus 21:22,23 in the Septuagint version, namely, between the destruction of the unformed and the formed fetus. Thus the author of the *Apostolic Constitutions*, a fourth-century compilation of ecclesiastical law of Syrian origin, bases the greater part of his seventh book on the *Didache* and declares: 'Thou shalt not procure abortion nor commit infanticide [*Did.* 2.2] for *everything that is formed* [cf. Exodus 21:23 LXX] and has received a soul from God, if it is slain, shall be avenged, as being unjustly destroyed.'[63] Both St. Ambrose (c.339-397), bishop of Milan, and St. John Chrysostom (c.347-407), bishop of Constantinople, condemn abortion, Ambrose denouncing rich men who destroy the fetus in the womb with 'parricidal drugs' (*parricidalibus sucis*) to avoid division of their estates among many children,[64] and Chrysostom rebuking those who frequent prostitutes and thereby encourage such women to destroy their unborn offspring for financial gain.[65] St. Jerome (331/347-420) speaks of tragic cases of consecrated Christian virgins who endeavour to conceal the guilt of fornication. 'Some even ensure barrenness by the help of potions, murdering human beings before they are fully conceived. Others, when they find they are with child as a result of their sin, practise abortion with drugs, and so frequently bring about their own death, taking with them to the lower world the guilt of three crimes: suicide, adultery against Christ, and child-murder.'[66]

Augustine (354-430), bishop of Hippo, the greatest and intellectually most influential of the early Latin theologians, agrees with the other Fathers. Because of the qualification in Exodus 21:22,23, Augustine was forced to make a distinction between the formed and the unformed fetus, and felt unable to regard the destruction of the unformed fetus as homicide.[67] This scriptural distinction inevitably led Augustine to ask the question: at what point does the human being begin to be alive in the womb, and is there even a sort of concealed life which is not as yet made evident by the movements of the living child? Augustine had some doubt as to whether human ingenuity could find an answer to this problem, which was of concern to him in the context of the theology of the resurrection. 'As for abortions which, although alive in the womb, died before birth, I dare neither affirm nor deny their resurrection. But if you include them among the number of the dead, I do not see how you can exclude them from the resurrection of the dead. . . . I cannot see how I can say that they do not belong to the resurrection of the dead, even if they died in their mother's womb.'[68] It was, no doubt, this uncertainty about the moment at which the fetus could be reckoned a human being which helped to condition Augustine's view of abortion, to which he is utterly opposed. In his treatise *On Marriage and Concupiscence*, written in 419/21-422, he denounces (characteristically) any indulgence of the sexual instinct which is not directed to the begetting of children and then goes on:

> Sometimes (*Aliquando*) this lustful cruelty or cruel lust goes so far as to employ drugs to cause sterility; and if this is ineffective it finds a way to destroy and expel fetuses conceived in the womb, willing its offspring to die before it lives [if the fetus is unformed] or, if it is already quickened in the womb [i.e. if it is already formed], to die before it is born. Very well then: if both parties are such [as to do this], they are not married; and if they were such from the beginning, they have come together not by wedlock but rather by debauchery. If however they are not both such, I make bold to say that either the woman is in some way the husband's harlot or the man the wife's adulterer.[69]

This passage from Augustine was to constitute the canon *Aliquando*, included in the great canonical collection called the *Decretum* or *Concordance of Discordant Canons* compiled by Gratian, 'the Father of the Science of Canon Law,' about 1140, which soon became a standard textbook and reference work.[70] Thus Augustine's teaching passed into Western Canon Law, supplemented by the teaching of Gratian himself, based on that of Jerome and Augustine, that abortion before the formation of the fetus was not equivalent to homicide.

However, in 1234 Pope Gregory IX, in his decretal collection, reproduced the canon *Si Aliquis*, derived from the *De Ecclesiastica Disciplina* of Regino of Prüm, and subsequently repeated by Burchard of Worms and Bartholomew of Exeter: 'If anyone for the sake of fulfilling lust or in meditated hatred does something to a man or a woman, or gives them to drink, so that he cannot generate or she conceive, or offspring be born, let it be held as homicide.'[71] So this canon, originally, it would seem, directed against attacks on adult fertility rather than the fetus itself,[72] passed into the law of the medieval Western Church,[73] and by its equation of abortion with homicide abolished the distinction between the formed and the unformed fetus, still maintained by the Augustinian-inspired canon *Aliquando*.

The chronological limits of our theme do not permit us to pursue our study further. In many respects the whole essay has been a documentation of the undeniable, and it may fairly be said that until the twentieth century no serious Christian of any denomination would have attended to defend abortion—if at all—except in the rarest and most exceptional circumstances. Furthermore, the secular legislation of most European countries on this issue accepted Christian teaching as a norm, and treated abortion as a criminal offence, so that in 1934 the Jesuit scholar, Franz Joseph Dölger, could quote with approval the judgement of M. Beth: 'Under the influence of the Catholic Church the defence of the life of the child was extended even to the embryo. Even today almost all modern legislation still maintains this point of view.'[74] By the 1980s the situation has completely changed, and almost all modern states have introduced legislation permitting abortion to a greater or lesser extent. With this radical chance of outlook has gone a correspondingly greater willingness to tolerate the deaths of physically or mentally handicapped infants, if their parents are unable or unwilling to face the heavy demands which the nurture of such children inevitably imposes. As a result, in a curious way, medical advance and social changes have caused to be heard sentiments and arguments which, to the historian of the Church in the Graeco-Roman world, have a curiously familiar ring. Thus, although the exposure of the unwanted infant is not permitted, it is widely held that the decision as to whether a seriously-handicapped baby is to live or to be allowed to die should rest with the parents, under medical guidance; and when in August 1981 a baby suffering from Down's Syndrome, whom her parents wished to be allowed to die, was made a ward of court at the request of a London borough council and subjected to an operation to ensure her survival, there were indignant protests from some quarters and the British Paediatric Association made clear its displeasure at the decision.[75] Abortion has been defended on the grounds of the freedom of the parent—though now it is the mother, not the father, who has the power of decision, the *patria potestas* of antiquity being superseded by a *potestas materna*.[76] The Roman legal view that the fetus is no more than part of the mother's viscera has been restated in terms of the subjective feelings of the pregnant woman.[77] In short, the claims made by traditional Christianity for an alleged right to life enjoyed by a human fetus or newborn child, which have for many centuries been taken for granted in western society, have been openly challenged and set aside.

It would be easy to denounce these arguments as being no more than the attempted justification of human selfishness—Augustine's 'lustful cruelty or cruel lust' excusing itself by argument—but to do so would be unfair to the advocates of abortion. Rather, their attitude should be seen as the product of an ethic which makes the avoidance of physical suffering the criterion for moral conduct and which, if it has to make a choice between the lives of two individuals, will favour the one with the greater capacity for suffering: the pregnant woman against the fetus, the parents against the handicapped child. In an extremely interesting article on the British social legislation of the 1960s, Mr Christie Davies has interpreted the parliamentary debates which it involved as a battle between what he calls moralism and causalism. The moralist position—which is indeed very typical of religious opponents of abortion—sees the issues involved in

terms of right and wrong: if an activity is evil, that in itself constitutes a ground for forbidding it. Causalism, on the other hand,
holds that if more harm is done by legally forbidding an activity
than by permitting it, then that activity should be permitted,
even if it is deemed wrong or immoral.[78] Causalism (in Davies's
words) 'is the lowest common denominator of morality, the only
possible language of communication between the diverse ideo-
logical groups to be found in Parliament'.[79] Inevitably, such an
outlook will be essentially a short-term negative utilitarianism,
concerned 'with the immediate and tangible consequences of the
law, with things that can be measured or easily demonstrated,'[80]
and its advocates will tend to embrace the principle that the avoidance of suffering without regard to moral status is the criterion
for legislation and so can, without logical inconsistency, oppose
capital punishment and approve abortion. 'The fetus can be sacrificed but not the murderer simply because its capacity for suffering is less. It cannot anticipate the moment of its demise, it has
no plans, expectations, relationships that would be suddenly,
finally and irreversibly disrupted. It cannot know the sufferings
which spring from human self-consciousness and awareness.'[81]

Such an outlook, particularly if it is supported by demands for
abortion based upon the freedom of a woman to determine her
own fertility, and of parents to reject a handicapped child, represents a return to the attitudes of the Graeco-Roman world, with
the practical advantage that the controlled demise and disposal of
the fetus or the neonate in the privacy of a hospital spares the
public the unpleasant spectacle of dying infants or their corpses
abandoned on the rubbish-heaps of cities, as they were apt to be
in the ancient world. Furthermore, on a deeper and more philosophical level of thought, arguments have been advanced that the
fetus, until it becomes sentient at a certain stage of its development within the womb, has no moral standing, with the result
that an abortion procured before this stage is no different from
contraception[82]—an argument which, although using different
terminology, reproduces the old Aristotelian distinction between
the formed and the unformed fetus, and enables the pre-sentient
fetus to be regarded as being simply parasitic upon the mother[83]
—a view which, in turn, provides a justification for abortion
which deflects in advance any equation of abortion with
infanticide.

Clearly, such an ethic is wholly opposed to the attitude of the Fathers of the Church towards abortion and infanticide; but it is worth considering the thought underlying the Fathers' condemnation. Of their condemnation there can be no question; and the grisly fate awaiting guilty parents after death is vividly depicted in popular apocryphal literature, like the *Apocalypses* of Peter and Paul. When, however, we come to examine the reasoning of the Fathers with regard to abortion, as opposed to their unanimous condemnation of the practice, we do not find unanimity. Tertullian might equate the destruction of the fetus at any stage of its development with homicide, but other theologians felt themselves constrained by the text of Scripture to admit a distinction between the formed and the unformed fetus, even if, like Basil of Caesarea, they declined to take this into account in assessing culpability.[84] One cannot therefore simply argue that the Fathers saw the embryo as a human being from the moment of its conception and based their condemnation of its destruction upon that assumption; their theology was, in fact, more varied than their denunciation.

Perhaps, at bottom, the patristic case against abortion turned upon the fact that the Fathers, unlike the pagans and their modern intellectual successors, had a long-term view of the fetus and its destiny. In his *City of God* St Augustine of Hippo discusses the question: will abortions have a place in the resurrection, even if they died in their mother's womb and will infants receive the body to which they would have grown if they had not died?[85] Speculation of this sort will strike most modern readers as being utterly futile; but it indicates Augustine's opinion that one cannot evaluate an individual simply from a particular point in time, but in terms of his potentialities and final destiny. If we apply this type of thinking to the fetus in the womb, we have to accept that an abortion at the present time deprives another potential human being of a life in the future. 'The central question in the abortion issue', L.W. Sumner has written, 'is not whether foetuses are human, but whether all human beings, including foetuses, have the same moral status.'[86] To this the patristic answer, and indeed the answer of traditional Christianity, is that they have; and Christians are required to recognize this moral status.

To say this is not to recommend a juridical attitude to the

problem of abortion on the part of the Church. The saying that hard cases make bad law is a lawyer's maxim, not a Christian's, and we should be grateful to Catholic moral theologians of the past, like John of Naples and Tomás Sanchez,[87] who explored and discussed the anomalous situations when an abortion may possibly be justified. Christianity is not, after all, a set of rules, but a common life within the body of Christ, which demands love and care for the individual as an individual, and not as a mere legal entity. The need for pastoral concern as opposed to legalism was early recognized in the Church. From the Council of Ancyra onwards, Christian pastors declined to punish abortion as if it were equivalent to voluntary homicide, as earlier discipline had done. 'But now we decree more humanely . . .' declared the Fathers of Ancyra, and this phrase regularly reappeared with the canon in conciliar legislation during the succeeding centuries.

A final point remains: to what extent are Christians, living in a post-Christian society like contemporary Britain, justified in trying to impose their own objections to abortion upon their non-Christian fellow-countrymen by law? The Fathers, once the alliance between Church and state brought about by the conversion of Constantine had become effective, were happy to welcome legislation forbidding pagan worship and practice. Today, most Christians would regard the support of freedom of religion for others as part of their own Christian duty and would hold that, in the field of private morality, the non-Christian should be allowed to follow his own conscience. The difficulty about applying these principles to abortion (and, by extension, to infanticide) is that we are here concerned, not only with one individual—the pregnant woman—but with the fetus, who must, at the very least, be regarded as an individual in potentiality, and who is therefore entitled, on the Christian view, to legal protection. A Christian cannot accept the view that in an abortion only the mother is involved and that the decision should, therefore, rest with her alone.

On the other hand, as a matter of practical politics in the Britain of the last two decades of the twentieth century, it seems all but impossible that any political party would support legislation that would effectively make abortion illegal. In such circumstances the best course for Christians, both as individuals and as members of their particular communions, would seem to be to bear positive witness to their own convictions of the wrongness of abortion and, on a practical level, to give all possible encouragement and practical help to women who, finding themselves pregnant against their will, may be tempted or in some cases be subjected to medical pressure to seek relief in an abortion.[88] Perhaps the strongest argument that the advocates of abortion can use against Christians is to assert that they are anxious to forbid abortion but not willing to give the women who ask for it the help and support which they require.[89] The Church of the Fathers was not, fundamentally, a Church of legislation and negation. It was a Church which offered comfort and support to its members within, while its philanthropy to those outside was recognized even by those who were most hostile to it.[90] If Christians seek to eradicate abortion, their most effective argument will not be by words but by active concern for those whose need impels them to demand it.

To all appearances the chances of ending the legal toleration of abortion in Britain would appear to be small. Attempts to control it by introducing parliamentary legislation have failed, owing to lack of time. The Labour Party is officially committed to maintaining it. For many people the practice is socially acceptable, and it is significant that a publication like *The Hospitals and Health Services Yearbook* of 1981 can list The Abortion Law Reform Association under the heading 'Hospital and Health Service Organizations'[91] while omitting any reference to anti-abortion bodies like The Society for the Protection of Unborn Children and Life. At the same time, we need not be too pessimistic, especially when we remember the long continuance of an abuse like the slave trade which, like abortion, represented a good deal of vested interest, before it was declared illegal in 1807, after the bill for its abolition had been introduced in the House of Commons, debated and defeated eleven times. The climate of public opinion on moral issues does change. A survey carried out in 1974-75 on the sexual attitudes of young people aged between sixteen and nineteen revealed that, 'contrary to what might have been expected, a greater proportion disapproved [of abortion] than approved. . . . The fact that over half the girls and over forty per cent of the boys expressed disapproval (and often horror) of abortion is an indication that young people are not encouraged to have sex because abortion is more easily available now.'[92] It would appear, in the light of such investigations, that efforts to promote the view that abortion is essentially an aspect of sexual conduct, not very different from contraception, are not proving wholly successful, perhaps because, whatever the advocates of abortion may urge, the legacy of nineteen centuries of Christianity, even rather indifferent Christianity, is not so easily discarded as they would wish. Human beings still find it difficult to regard the fetus as having no claim upon their compassion.

NOTES

[1]   *Bibliography*: The fundamental articles for any study of abortion in the classical world are Franz Joseph Dölger, 'Das Lebensrecht des ungeborenen Kindes und die Fruchtabtreibung in der Bewertung der heidnischen und christlichen Antike,' *Antike und Christentum* iv (1934), pp.1-61, corrected on points of detail by J.H. Waszink in *Reallexikon für die Antike und Christentum*, Bd I (Stuttgart 1950), art. 'Abtreibung,' cols. 55-60, and John T. Noonan, Jr., 'An almost Absolute Value in History,' *The Morality of Abortion. Legal and Historical Perspectives*, ed. by J. T. Noonan (Cambridge, Mass. 1970), pp.1-59. My debt to these three authors will be obvious to anyone familiar with them.

    On exposure there is considerably more material, since most histories of the Graeco-Roman world refer to it. Besides the works of Zimmern (note[5]), Carcopino (note[6]) and Hands (note[10]), consult William Tarn and G. T. Griffith, *Hellenistic Civilisation*, 3rd ed. (London 1966), pp.100-02. Raphael Taubenschlag, *The Law of Graeco-Roman Egypt in the Light of the Papyri 332 B.C.—640 A.D.*, 2nd ed. (Warsaw 1955), p.138 n.[26] and Jean-Paul Audet, *La Didachè. Instructions des Apôtres* (Paris 1958), pp.288-9 provide comprehensive bibliographies.

[2]   Tert., *Apology* 9.6-8. Tr. by F. A. Wright, *Fathers of the Church. A Selection from the Writings of the Latin Fathers* (London 1928), pp.30-31, slightly modified.

[3]   'Viewed coldbloodedly . . . infanticide is an efficient method of limiting fertility in that it endangers the health of the mother less than an abortion procured in unhygienic surroundings and need be much less often carried out since a child unfortunate enough to die in this way will have gone to full term, whereas an abortion takes up only a few months of a woman's fertile period' (E. A. Wrigley, *Population and History* (London 1969), p.126.

[4]   See Dio Chrysostom, *Or.*15.8: '. . . And the other man replied: 'Yes, I know that freeborn women often palm off other persons' children as their own on account of their childlessness, when they are unable to conceive

children themselves, because each one wishes to keep her own husband and her home, while at the same time they do not lack the means to support the children; but in the case of slave women, on the other hand, some destroy the child before birth and others afterwards, if they can do so without being caught, and yet sometimes even with the connivance of their husbands, that they may not be involved in trouble by being compelled to raise children in addition to their enduring slavery' (Loeb ed. Vol.II, p.151).

5 Alfred Zimmern, *The Greek Commonwealth*, 5th ed. (Oxford 1961), p .331.

6 Jérome Carcopino, *Daily Life in Ancient Rome*, E.T. by E. O. Lorrimer (London: Peregrine Books 1964), p.90.

7 *Ad Diognetum* 5.6.

8 Strabo, XVII.2.5 (C 824): 'One of the customs most zealously observed by the Egyptians is this, that they rear every child that is born, and circumcise the males and excise the females, as is also customary among the Jews' (Loeb ed. Vol. VIII, p.153).

9 P.Oxy. 744, tr. by George Milligan, *Selections from the Greek Papyri* (Cambridge 1910), pp.32-33. (I omit the mysterious word *pollapollon*, whose meaning is uncertain.)

10 As does Adolf Deissmann, *Licht vom Osten*, 4th ed. (Tübingen 1923), p.136. See the comment of A. R. Hands, *Charities and Social Aid in Greece and Rome* (London 1968), p.70: 'A whole series of quotations gathered by Stobaeus suggests that the "cruelty" shown to those children who were exposed was viewed by parents rather as loving concern that those who *were* allowed to survive should not have to endure poverty.'

11 Poseidippus, *Hermaphroditus*, ed. Meinecke, *Fr.Com.Gr.* 4, p.156, quoted by W. L. Newman, *The Politics of Aristotle* Vol.III (Oxford 1902), p.474.

12 Dio Chrysostom, *Or.* 15.8. See above, note [4].

13 *Codex Theodosianus* IX.14.1: 'Si quis necandi infantis piaculum aggressus aggressa sit, erit capitale istud malum. . . . *Interpretatio:* Sive vir sive mulier infantem necaverit, rei homicidii *teneantur.*' Constantine the Great had already issued two laws in 315 and 322 respectively, providing for relief for poor parents from the imperial treasury, to save them from infanticide or the sale of their children into slavery (*CT* XI.27.1 and 2).

14 Paulus, *Digest* XXV.3.4: 'Paulus libro secundo sententiarum: *Necare videtur non tantum is qui partum praefocat, sed et is qui abicit et qui alimonia denegat et is qui publicis locis misericordiae causa exponit, quam ipse non habet.*'

15 Tert., *Adversus Nationes* I, p.153: 'For if we [Christians] are infanticides in one sense, you also can hardly not be deemed such in another sense; because, although you are forbidden by the laws to slay new-born infants, it so happens that no laws are evaded with more impunity or greater safety, and with the deliberate knowledge of the public, and the suffrages of this

entire age' (Tr. in *The Ante-Nicene Fathers*, Vol.III, p.123, slightly modified).

16 Seneca, *De Ira* 1.15.2: 'Mad dogs we knock on the head; the fierce and savage ox we slay; sickly sheep we put to the knife to keep them from infecting the flock; unnatural progeny we destroy; we drown even children, who at birth are weakly and abnormal' (Loeb ed., Vol.I, p.145).

17 *Should every child that is born be raised?* Text in Cora E. Lutz, 'The Roman Socrates,' *Yale Classical Studies* X (1947), pp.96-101. See M. P. Charlesworth, *Five Men: Character Studies from the Roman Empire* (Martin Classical Lectures Vol. VI) (Cambridge, Mass. 1936), p.46.

18 Plato, *Resp.* V, p.9 (461 BC).

19 Aristotle, *Pol.* VII, pp.xii, 15 (1335 B).

20 Aristotle, *Historia Animalium* VII, p.3 (538 A).

21 Basil, *Ep.*188, Canon 2: 'A woman who deliberately destroys a fetus is answerable for murder. And any fine distinction as to its being completely formed or unformed is not admissible amongst us' (Loeb ed., Vol.III,21). Cf. Canon 8: '. . . And so women who give drugs that cause abortion are themselves murderers as well as those who take the poisons that kill the fetus' (Ibid., p.35).

22 *Stoicorum Veterum Fragmenta*, ed. Arnim, ii. no.806. See Dölger, art. cit. note[1] above, p.21.

23 See Charlesworth, op.cit. note[17] above.

24 *Digest* XXXV.2.9.1: 'partus nondum editus homo non recte fuisse dicitur.'

25 *Digest* XXV.4.1.1: 'partus enim antequam edatur, mulieris portio est vel viscerum.'

26 Cicero, *Pro Cluentio* 11.32.

27 *Digest* XLVII.11.4: 'Marcianus libro primo regularum: *Divus Severus et Antonius rescripserunt eam, quae data opera abegit, a praeside in temporale exilium dandam: indignum enim videri potest impune eam maritum liberis fraudisse.*'

28 *Hippocratic Oath*: '. . . I will use treatment to help the sick according to my ability and judgement, but never with a view to injury and wrong-doing. Neither will I administer a poison to anybody when asked to do so, nor will I suggest such a course. Similarly I will not give to a woman a pessary to cause abortion. . . .' (Loeb ed., Vol.I, p.299).

29 Tert., *De Anima* 25: 'in ipso adhuc utero infans trucidatur necessaria crudelitate, cum in exitu obliquatus denegat partum matricida, ni moriturus.'

30 Seneca, *De Consolatione ad Helviam* 16.1: '. . . never have you, in the manner of other women whose only recommendation lies in their beauty, tried to conceal your pregnancy, as if an unseemly burden, nor have you

crushed the hope of children that were being nurtured in your body' (Loeb ed., Vol.II, p.473).

31 H. J. Rome, *A Handbook of Latin Literature*, 2nd ed. (London 1954), p.326.

32 Ovid, *Amores* II. 13. 7-15.

33 Ibid., II. 14. 9-10, 19-20.

34 Clement, *Eclogae Propheticae* 50.1-3. See Michel Spanneut, *Le Stoicisme des Pères de l'Église* (Paris 1957), pp.191-7.

35 See Dölger, art.cit. note[1] above, pp.3-6.

36 Philo, *De Specialibus Legibus* iii. 108-09 (Loeb ed., Vol.VII, p.545).

37 Ibid., 117 (pp.549, 551).

38 Ibid., 118 (pp.551, 553).

39 Josephus, *Contra Apionem* ii. 202 (Loeb ed., Vol.I, pp.373, 375).

40 See Plato, *Theaetetus* 149D.

41 See Immanuel Jakobvits, *Jewish Medical Ethics*, 2nd ed. (New York 1975), p.274: 'On abortion generally the predominant view prevails limiting its sanction to cases involving a grave anticipated hazard to the mother, whether physical or psychological.' See also *Encyclopaedia Judaica*, Vol.2, art. 'Abortion,' cols. 98-101. In 1942, when the Germans had decreed that any woman becoming pregnant in the Kovno ghetto should be put to death, together with her offspring, Rabbi Ephraim Oshry decided that abortion was permissible, in order to save the pregnant woman's life (col. 100).

42 *Did.* 2.2; cf.5.2.

43 *Barn.* 20.2.

44 Athenag., *Supplicatio* 35.6. Tr. by William R. Schoedel (Oxford 1972), p.85.

45 Clem. Alex., *Protrepticus* II, x.96.1.

46 *Apocalypse of Peter* 8. Tr. in E. Hennecke, *New Testament Apocrypha*, E.T. by R. McL. Wilson, Vol.II (London 1965), pp.674-5.

47 *Apocalypse of Paul* 40 (Hennecke II, p.784).

48 *Sibyllines* II, lines 279-292 (Hennecke II, p.717).

49 Tert., *Apol.*9.8.

50 Tert., *De Anima* 27; 52.3.

51 Tert., *De Anima* 37.2.

52 Minucius Felix, *Octavius* 30.2,3 (Loeb., ed. p.407).

53 Cyprian, *Ep.* 52.ii.3 (*CSEL* iii (2), p.619). Dölger (art. cit., p.55) identifies the offender with the deacon Felicissimus; Noonan (art. cit., p.14) corrects

this, but unfortunately substitutes the name of the austere schismatic Novatian for that of Novatus.

54 Labbe, *Concilia* Tom.I, col.1493. In view of the doubts raised by Dölger (art. cit., pp.55,56) I have not included canons 63 and 68 of the Council of Elvira (*c.*305) in the anti-abortion legislation of the early Church.

55 See above, note[21].

56 Ivo of Chartres, *Decretum* X, c.181 (*PL* clxi, 744 CD).

57 Bartholomew, *Penitential*, canon 56, ed. Adrian Morey, *Bartholomew of Exeter, Bishop and Canonist* (Cambridge 1937), p.222.

58 The Council of Worms of 868 did enact a canon (35) against abortion (Labbe X, 462); but this is not the one quoted.

59 Burchard of Worms, *Decretum* XVII, c.57 (*PL* cxl, 933 B).

60 Regino of Prüm, *De Ecclesiastica Disciplina* II, 89: 'Si aliquis causa explendae libidinis, vel odii meditatione, ut non ex eo soboles nascatur, homini aut mulieri aliquid fecerit, vel ad potandum dederit, ut non possit generare aut concipere, ut homicida teneatur' (*PL* cxl, 933 B).

61 Bartholomew, op.cit., c.56 (ed. Morey, p.222).

62 Ibid.: 'Si qua mulier abortum fecerit voluntarie, tribus annis poeniteat' (*PL* cxl, 934 B).

63 *Didascalia et Constitutiones Apostolorum* VII. iii. 2. Tr. by Philip Schaff, *The Oldest Church Manual called the* Teaching of the Twelve Apostles (New York 1885), p.264, slightly modified.

64 Ambrose, *Hexameron* V. xviii. 58 (*CSEL* xxxii[1], p.184).

65 John Chrysostom, *In Ep. ad Rom. Hom.* 24,4 (PG lx, pp.626-7).

66 Jerome, *Ep.*22,13. Tr. by F. A. Wright, Loeb ed., p.79.

67 Aug., *Quaest. in Heptateuchum II: Quaest. in Exodo* xxi.80 (*CSEL* xxviii[2], p.148).

68 Aug., *De Civitate Dei* XXII, xiii. Tr. by J. W. C. Wand, *St Augustine's City of God* (London 1963), p.400.

69 Aug., *De Nuptiis et Concupiscentia* I. xv. 17 (*CSEL* xlii, p.230).

70 Gratian, *Decretum* II. 32. 2. 7 (ed. Rome 1582, cols. 2109-10).

71 Gregory, *Decretales* V. 12. 5. Tr. by Noonan, art. cit., p.21.

72 This canon comes under the general heading: '*De eo qui hominem castraverit.*' Regino has a series of canons (63 = Ancyra canon 21; 64; 65; 66 [*PL* cxxxii, 297 D—298 B] specifically directed against abortion. Canon 69 (= Buchard, III, c.200 [*PL* cxl, 712 BC]) provides for the exposition of illegitimate infants at the church door for adoption by one of the faithful as an arrangement to discourage the sins of abortion and infanticide.

73 James B. Nelson, *Human Medicine* (Minneapolis 1973), p.35.

74 Dölger, art. cit., p.61.

75 See *The Times*, 19 August 1981, p.2. Dr David Murray, secretary of the BPA, is there quoted as saying: 'I think we must try and keep this [namely, the decision to give or withhold treatment to a severely-handicapped baby] a private affair between doctor and parents.'

76 So the United States Supreme Court in *Roe v. Wade* (1973), cited in Nelson, op.cit. note[73] above, p.49. See Nelson's comment on the rights of the father, pp.54, 55.

77 Rachel Conrad Wahlberg, 'The Woman and the fetus: "One Flesh"?' *The Christian Century* (8 September 1971), p.1045 ff. cited in Nelson, op. cit., p.49.

78 Christie Davies, 'Moralists, Causalists, Sex, Law and Morality' in *Changing Patterns of Sexual Behaviour*, edd. W. H. G. Armytage, R. Chester and John Peel (London 1980), pp.13,14.

79 Ibid., p.38.

80 Ibid., p.14.

81 Ibid., p.21.

82 See Peter Singer, 'Conception and Misconception' [a review of L. W. Sumner, *Abortion and Moral Theory* (Princeton University Press)], *The Times Literary Supplement* No 4,100 (30 October 1981), p.1267.

83 See L. W. Sumner, *The Times Literary Supplement* No 4,105 (4 December 1981), p.1419, replying to criticisms by Martin W. Helgesen, *TLS* No 4,103 (20 November 1981), p.1367. Sumner takes his definition of a parasite from *Stedman's Medical Dictionary*: 'An organism that lives on or in another, and draws its nourishment therefrom.' In discussion of abortion, however, the word parasite, as Helgesen remarks, is 'an emotionally charged pejorative' and to be avoided.

84 See above, note[21].

85 Aug., *City of God* XXII, xiii, xiv.

86 Sumner, *TLS* No 4,105 (4 December 1981), p.1419.

87 See Noonan, art. cit., pp.26-30.

88 That persuasion, which may amount in certain cases to actual pressure, is exercised, is known to the writer from particular examples.

89 Such an argument will not, of course, be used by those who see abortion as a form of liberation of the individual from the constraints of a tyrannous society. See, for example, Victoria Greenwood and Jock Young, *Abortion in Demand* (London 1976), pp.92, 93: '. . . to detect weaknesses [in the abortionist case] is not to solve them. For there is precious little that organizations such as SPUC would provide for women or the poor other than charity. . . . It is by welding free abortion on demand to the whole range of changes necessary to generate genuine freedom of choice that we can transcend reformism.'

90 See the testimony of an anti-Christian like Julian the Apostate, Ep.22: 'For it is disgraceful that, when no Jew has to beg and the impious Galilaeans [i.e. the Christians] support not only their own poor, but ours as well, all men see that our people lack aid from us' (130 D Loeb ed. Vol.III, pp.70, 71): *Fragment of a Letter to a Priest:* 'For when it came about that the poor were neglected and overlooked by the [pagan] priests, then I think the impious Galilaeans observed the fact and devoted themselves to philanthropy. And credit they win from such practices' (305 BC Loeb ed. Vol.II, pp.836, 837). See the comment of E. R. Dodds, *Pagan and Christian in an Age of Anxiety* (Cambridge 1965), pp.137-8: 'Within the [Christian] community there was human warmth; someone was interested in [the lonely and the rootless], both here and hereafter. It was therefore not surprising that the earliest and the most striking advances of Christianity were made in the great cities—in Antioch, in Rome, in Alexandria. Christians were in a more than formal sense "members one of another." I think that was a cause, perhaps the strongest single cause, of the spread of Christianity.'

91 *The Hospitals and Health Services Yearbook*, ed. N. W. Chaplin (London 1981), p.474: 'The Association was formed in 1936 with the object of introducing abortion to reduce the mortality and morbidity resulting from criminal abortions. The Association is now seeking through the "A Woman's Right to Choose" Campaign to obtain a change in legislation to allow abortion on request and an improvement in NHS facilities.'

92 Christine Farrell, 'Social Attitudes and Behaviour of Young People' in op. cit. note[78] above, pp.67, 69.

Epilogue

6

Again: Who Is a Person?

OLIVER O'DONOVAN

'And he, desiring to justify himself, said to Jesus, "And who is my neighbour?" ' Moral theologians have never tired of pointing out that Jesus did not answer the question in the terms in which it was put. The student of the law knew that he had an obligation to care for a certain class of person, called 'neighbours'; accordingly, he asked for criteria by which he would recognize members of this class. Jesus offered him no criteria, but told a story illustrating how someone discharged the obligation of neighbour-love—someone who might quite plausibly have been held to be outside the category, 'neighbour', because he was not a Jew. 'Which of the three, do you think, proved neighbour to the man who fell among the robbers?' 'The one who showed mercy on him.'

There are at least three ways in which the answer of Jesus defeats the hidden presuppositions of the lawyer's question. In the first place, Jesus' answer clearly implies a 'universalist' doctrine of neighbourhood, whereas the lawyer, we must suppose, had in mind some kind of racial restriction. That is the most obvious, and perhaps least dramatic challenge that Jesus makes to his questioner. In the second place, Jesus' story shows *how* we identify our neighbour; from our active engagement with him in caring for him, sympathizing with him, protecting him. There is, in other words, an epistemology implied in the story; at the *end* of this engagement we can say that the neighbourhood of the two men has become apparent. It would never have become clear *whether* a Samaritan and a Jew could be neighbours, if the Samaritan, like the lawyer, had waited for the question to be answered speculatively before he attended to the Jew at the roadside. The truth of neighbourhood is known in engagement; we act in commitment to someone *as* a neighbour, and thus *prove* the neighbourhood. In the third place, this is a story about how a Jew learned who his neighbour was. He learned it, not by serving him, but by being served by him. And this, perhaps, is the most scandalous element in Jesus' story: that a Jew could *need* a Samaritan as his neighbour, that the natural relation (as he saw it) of patron and client could be reversed, and that he would solve the speculative problem about Samaritans as neighbours not even by caring for a Samaritan in need, but by being cared for, in his need, by a Samaritan.

And who, then, is a person?

The term 'person' is clearly intended to be a universal term, in the way that 'neighbour'. is. The question has already taken cognizance of the first challenge that Jesus offered to the lawyer. My case is a very simple one: that the question about 'personhood' has to take notice also of the second and third challenges which Jesus made. That is to say: (*a*) that we can recognize someone as a person only from a stance of *prior moral commitment* to treat him or her as a person, since the question of what constitutes a person can never be answered speculatively; and (*b*) that we know someone as a person as that person is disclosed in his or her personal relations to us, that is, as we know ourselves to be not simply the subject of our own attention to the other, but to be the object of the other's attention to us. On the basis of point (*a*) my account of personhood will be called (and deserves to be called) 'existentialist'—and it is no worse for that, but simply recognizes a fundamental truth about human knowledge which could be found in the New Testament long before anyone declared that it was 'existentialist', namely, that certain kinds of knowledge are given to us only within an active commitment of faith and obedience: 'If any man's will is to do his will, he shall know whether the teaching is from God' (John 7:17). On the basis of point (*b*), however, we can claim to be safe from that solipsistic tendency into which popular existentialism has too often degenerated. We are not saying that personhood is *conferred* upon the object simply by our willingness to treat him or her as a person. Rather the opposite: we *discover* the personhood of the other by his personal dealings with us. We hold, therefore, to an existentialist *anthropology*. What is required of us is a commitment to be open to the other *as another human agent*, to be open to interaction with him in every form. The term 'person', too, must carry with it this implication of the old term 'neighbour', that we find ourselves with somebody 'next to' us, like us, equal to us, acting upon us as we upon him, as much a subject to whom we become object as he is object to our subject. And this presupposes a doctrine of human nature, and an understanding that we who encounter the equal and opposite other are, with him, mankind.

I

In the first place, then, there are no 'criteria of personhood' by which a person could be recognized independently of, or prior to, *personal engagement*. To say this is to say something about humanity: that members of our species are known (at least to one another) *in a way* that members of other animal species are not known. We may recognize a duck abstractly, by simple observation, and distinguish it from a goose. In the same way, of course, we may distinguish a human being from an elephant; but such observational recognition falls short of the kind of knowledge that it is appropriate for one human being to have of another. And, notoriously, it does nothing to answer the moral questions about our fellow human beings which are posed for us by medical technology. When we ask whether someone in an irreversible coma is a 'person' or not, it does no good to answer that he is not an elephant. We want to know whether he still is that same human agent, with whom we have engaged as fellow agents in the business of life, and to whom we therefore owe a brotherly loyalty, or whether he is no longer 'he'. And the point I wish to make is that no conceivable set of purely observational criteria can answer that question positively or negatively for us. It might seem that we could answer it negatively, by adducing certain information about his brain-activity (which is not what it was when we used to meet him for lunch and discuss politics). It might seem that we could answer it positively, by showing that the vital functions of respiration and heartbeat are as spontaneously active as they used to be when he tasted wine and drew on his pipe. But both answers would miss the point: it was not his brain that we conversed with about the by-elections. It was he, the agent, the person; and although there would be no possibility of such engagement *without* the functioning brain, respiration and heartbeat, what we met and talked with was not simply the sum of those functions, but another category of subject altogether.

We met *him*—I say 'the person', but it is very important not to think that 'the person' is another *kind* of constituent, like 'the brain' or 'the heart', only different. It would be quite wrong, for example, to say that we met 'the mind'. What we met, simply, was 'Michael', the human being as irreducibly individual, irreplaceable, a member of a species, certainly, but not accounted for simply as 'an instance of kind X', but only as *himself*. To all this the word 'person' points. It is, therefore, from a logical point of view, a category mistake to try to demonstrate the presence or absence of a person by proving that this or that biological or neurological function is present or absent. It is a category mistake to say that a new conceptus cannot be a person until there is brain activity; it is a category mistake to say that it must be a person because there is an individual genetic structure. (I shall be defending a different use of this genetic evidence in a minute; for the moment I merely remark on the impropriety of this use.) For, whatever criteria we take, we end up by reducing the notion of personhood to that one constituent of human functioning.

It has seemed to some that they could evade the implications of this categorical difference by treating personhood as an epiphenomenon supervening upon the presence of biological and neurological functions, and so depending upon them without, nevertheless, being reducible to them. But our thought cannot grasp 'the person', in his unique particularity, by thinking along this route. The most that it can reach is a group of second-order capacities, different in kind from the biological or neurological functions, but no less generic than they are. It can reach what we call 'personality', which is the cluster of behavioural and relational attributes which characteristically belong to human beings as a kind. It is a common misunderstanding of talk about persons to think that it is interchangeable with talk about personality—as though the difference between the concrete and the abstract meant nothing—or with talk about some aspect of personality, such as the capacity for relationship. But in speaking of the human person we are not speaking of any kind of capacity nor of any kind of attribute. Our argument has not been that we can know persons by *observing* their capacity for relationship. We have said that we know them *in* relationship, which is to say, when we abandon the observer's stance altogether and commit ourselves to treating them *as* persons. Of course, persons are intended for relationship, and will therefore (barring accidents) develop the personal attributes and capacities. But that is a very different thing from taking these attributes as a supposedly objective criterion for determining their status as persons. Personality *discloses* personhood; it does not constitute it. Personal attributes develop, as self-consciousness develops; but persons do not develop, for they are not in the category of quality but of substance.

There is a sermon by Austin Farrer which opens with an account of how he visited a friend who was in an irrecoverable coma; he spoke his name and took his hand, and was profoundly moved to feel the dying man's hand close firmly upon his own in a responsive grasp. But sadly, he reflected, the appearance of relationship was deceptive. The grasp was to be explained as the spontaneous response of the local nerves in the palm of the hand, habituated by years of handshaking; the friend himself was too far gone to know his name or respond to a touch. Now, I put this observation to a neurosurgeon friend of mine, and he was quite uncomprehending. To him it was far from obvious that a deeply comatose person could not hear and respond in some way, and he himself would never discount any such sign, however remote, of awareness. Like many of us when we become fascinated by medical explorations of consciousness, Austin Farrer tried to 'know too much'. Of course, this comatose person's response was not unambiguous; we may well wonder what to make of it, since from an observer's point of view it is quite inconclusive. Farrer's sermon goes on to talk of babies' smiles and wind. Again, what we see is inconclusive; we don't know that a baby is smiling, but we don't know that it is not. Personal presence emerges out of hiddenness, through ambiguous signs, to the point of clear disclosure, and then retreats into ambiguity and hiddenness at the end. There is no sign of behaviour of which we can say, 'There he is present! There he has gone!'—short of death itself, of course, and even there there are ambiguities too obvious to be mentioned. All we can do is *act personally*, as person or as friend.

The importance of this, when applied to the question of human life in its beginnings, the unborn child from conception to birth, is that it allows us to acknowledge the *mysteriousness* of what it is that lives in the womb. No one, I suppose, can have been the parent of a child without experiencing bafflement and amazement at the incomprehensibility of what thought encounters there. It is certainly not what we normally encounter when we engage with some object as a 'person'. Parents have to go *beyond the phenomenon,* and, at first almost playfully, attribute person-hood to the living being in the womb—and this playful projection continues in some measure even after birth, as we see in the case of smiles and wind. But it would be quite wrong to imagine that this was simply a sentimental and arbitrary embroidery on some otherwise—specifiable cold sober 'facts' about the fetus. Nobody knows any cold sober facts; they merely observe the ambiguous phenomenon. This commitment of the parents to going beyond the phenomenon, treating the fetus as a baby, and then the newborn baby as a person, is actually *necessary*, if they are to care properly for it and if the baby is ever to develop those 'personal' characteristics which are not themselves personhood but com-municate it. Furthermore, it is not arbitrary to think that the fruit of the human womb will, given the right care, develop to the point of evincing personhood through personal characteristics. Parents who do this know what the natural goal of a pregnancy is, and act in expectation of that goal's being reached. In their commitment to that goal, their engagement with the unborn child as their baby, the possibility arises of their knowing their child as a person.

But what is true of the parents in particular has to be true of the whole community. All those who assist in the pregnancy (medically or otherwise) are equally committed to welcoming the new life. And those who have no involvement with *this* pregnancy are nevertheless encouraged to see it sympathetically from the same point of view, and by so doing learn the attitudes which will be important to them when and if they are parents. The commitment of parenting, in other words, is not a private and particular commitment only of *these* parents to *this* fetus, but a generic commitment of a community and its culture to personal care for fetuses in general. This commitment is important for the community's ability to recognize and welcome new members, and will be reflected subsequently in its care for children. Only a very confused culture, such as ours is presently, can arbitrarily treat one fetus in one way and another in another. The confusion must be resolved into a general cultural attitude to the unborn human. And if that attitude does not arise from the practice of parenting, where will it arise from?

I take the practice of *experimenting on embryos* as the clearest indication of what the alternative attitude to the unborn child is. Abortion as such does not express a decisive concept of the fetus; it is the mere *refusal* of parenthood, and can be defended sometimes as the disposal of an impersonal piece of tissue and sometimes as the overruling of one person's rights in favour of another's. Once we confront experiment, however, the philosophy is quite explicit: an embryo is manipulable tissue, which has the double advantage to the researcher of being at one and the same time human tissue, with a high degree of individual organization, and non-personal.

Once again, this philosophy goes beyond the phenomenon, and commits itself in action to a view of the embryo which cannot be demonstrated objectively. Non-personhood is every bit as unsusceptible of proof as personhood. The philosophy is demanded not by the phenomena of human beginnings but by the internal requirements of the commitment to scientific experiment itself. Experiment objectifies, assigns its subject to the status of "thing"—that is the logic of the undertaking. This does not in itself invalidate all experiment on human beings, but it does require a careful structure of symbolic safeguards—requirements of informed consent etc.—which exist to remind us all that the experimenter's perspective on the human subject is an abstraction, and potentially a dangerous one. No comparable safeguards exist in experiment on human embryos, nor could they be introduced without abolishing all useful research. We may therefore regard as purely speculative any suggestions about kinds of research which might be compatible with treating the embryo as a person, and simply say that for practical purposes experiment embodies and requires the decision not to treat it so. And that decision arises from the practice, and not vice versa.

We have to choose, then, between the alternative practices of scientific experiment and parenting as providing rival matrices for the commitment we have to unborn children as a class. This choice cannot be arbitrated existentially, but only on the basis of what is true about the world. In demanding that our common attitude should be formed by the commitment to parenthood, not by the commitment to scientific knowledge (for all the goods of mastery of disease which it promises us), we base ourselves on the truth that those whom we treat as persons when they are yet unborn, become *known* to us as persons when they are children; and that this truth is utterly hidden from us by the alternative practice. The fundamental incompatibility of these two perspectives is ultimately expressed as the decision either to know human beings personally, or not to know them so. The decision to 'play God'—to reidentify the human object—is also, and inescapably, a decision *not* to 'play man', to close ourselves off from the modes of mutual knowledge which essentially belong to the community of mankind.

II

Having said that discerning persons is a matter of commitment to moral engagement, we must add a second point: there are criteria of *appropriateness* for our engaging with other beings as persons in fidelity. It might be thought that the doctrine that we *know* persons only as we *treat* them as persons opened the door to all kinds of fantasy. What do we make, for example, of people who treat their pets or their plants as persons? Certainly the response they get is ambiguous, but that we allowed to be no obstacle; so is the response from the comatose man or the newborn baby ambiguous, but it is appropriate, nevertheless, to commit ourselves to them. Is it equally appropriate to commit ourselves to our plants? No; for, as we made it clear in the beginning, our existential commitment is founded on an anthropology. The commitment to the other is rationally justified because he and we are alike mankind. It is appropriate to commit oneself in engagement with mankind, as it is not with plants; which is not to say that some kind of commitment may not be appropriate also in dealing with plants, but not the kind of commitment that treats them as persons.

'But this,' someone may protest, 'simply begs the whole question. We started off asking whether certain doubtful beings—comatose patients and unborn babies—were really human beings in the full sense of being persons, and you told us that we would discover whether they were only if we assumed that they were and committed ourselves accordingly. Now you tell us that we must, after all, make up our minds *in advance* whether someone is a human being before we know whether to commit ourselves.' The appearance of circularity here is, however, only momentary. For we said also that there was a purely observational level at which we could 'know' human beings and distinguish them from elephants in the same way that we know ducks and distinguish them from geese. This is not knowing 'humanely'—that is as a human being *ought* to know another human being—but it is a form of knowledge, a knowledge of the human *phenomenon* which can render intelligible and appropriate the commitment to treating someone 'as a person'. The question then becomes: what are the criteria for discerning the human *phenomenon*? What is the human 'appearance', or human 'face', which invites us to commit ourselves to it in expectation and hope of meeting the human 'person'? But this question in turn cannot be answered simply as it stands, for phenomena themselves develop and unfold in time; the more one investigates an object, the more the phenomenon of that object unfolds. Take, for example, a famous shock-scene in Bergman's film *The Seventh Seal*. The hero approaches from behind a figure seated, slightly crouched, upon a rock, and taps him on the shoulder. As he does so, the figure slumps over and his head lurches round at an unnatural angle, to reveal that his eyes have been picked out and that it is nothing but a rotted corpse. The initial phenomenon of a living human being has quickly developed into something quite different. So we might frame the question in this way: how far into the phenomenon do we have to go before we have a sufficient basis for recognizing a human being to whom we may show humane fidelity?

But even in this form the question is misleading. The hero was not *wrong* to think he saw a living human being. That is what makes the shock shocking. It was perfectly appropriate for him to tap this figure on the shoulder, as one might arrest the attention of someone taking a nap. It would not have been appropriate for him to *go on* treating that figure as a living human being; but he had sufficient warrant to *approach* him in that way. It would have been inappropriate, indeed morally wicked, for him to transfix him with an arrow like a beast of prey, for such phenomenal evidence as he had suggested that he had to deal with a living man. So we need to get away from any form of the question which implies that there is a level of proof to be reached before we have warrant to interact with someone as a human being. Rather, the initial appearance of the human form is immediate, and immediately commands a committed humane response. If that appearance then breaks down and turns into something else, then we recognize we have made a mistake and abandon our 'committed' response. But we respond to the 'human face', the immediate self-presentation of humanity, and not to any measure of proof.

Consider the following scenario. The obstetrician cuts the umbilical cord, and the nurse washes the baby, weighs it, takes measures to protect it against infection, wraps it in a blanket to keep it warm; and then, of course, the parents talk to it, call it by its name, try to attract its attention, console its cries. But then the baby shows signs of being in trouble, and in a few minutes dies. It was pointless talking to it, calling it by its name, attracting its attention, for its eyes were sightless, its ears without hearing. But in the first moments it appeared normal. And when we say that the parents were right to *treat* it as a normal child until they knew it was *not* a normal child, we are not merely recommending that one should be on the safe side when in doubt. We are saying that the *only* proper response to the human appearance is the humane response. There could not be any question of *doubt* until the first deviant phenomena occurred; to profess doubt earlier than that would be the purest bad faith. The immediate appearance of a child was a quite sufficient warrant for commitment in those initial moments. (Does this example, perhaps, give us a paradigm for how we may think about natural fetal wastage by spontaneous abortion?)

To say that we respond to the 'immediate' appearance of a human being does not mean that we cannot learn to discern the human appearance more accurately. The first explorers who encountered pigmy peoples may have been in some justifiable doubt as to whether this was the human race or not. Today nobody could be justified in professing doubt on the matter. Many of us might make the mistake of supposing that someone was dead, when the skilled eye of a physician would suspect a coma. We can, in other words, learn to trace the generic patterns of the human phenomenon and identify some appearances— which lie outside our common experience—as belonging properly to the phenomenon of humanity and others as not doing so. This point is of great importance in assessing the claim on our attention made by the human embryo.

Earlier generations had perfectly legitimate difficulties in recognizing an unborn child (in embryo stage) as a human being. The discontinuities of appearance were striking, and, of course, the embryo was never observed alive. Consequently they hypothesized a moment of 'animation' in which this strange body was transformed and brought to life by the coming of the soul. We may compare this kind of thinking to early anthropological speculations about the Bantu races, which tried to show essential discontinuities with the Caucasian races. Subsequent scientific exploration of the phenomena has discredited the impression of such discontinuities. Similarly, scientific study of embryology has laid to rest the notion of a major physiological discontinuity in human development between embryo and fetal stage. Genetic studies have, on the other hand, indicated a major discontinuity at conception, when the parental genotypes re-form into a new gnome, the distinct endowment of the new conceptus. (This has meant, not only that the history of the embryo/fetus can no longer be conceived as including a moment of 'animation', but that it can no longer be extended back to include the history of the sperm before conception.)

Our generation cannot avoid the implications of this knowledge. Our recognition of the human face is improved, and we can now see it in the embryo, even in the invisible blastocyst and zygote, where our ancestors could not. This means that pre-modern speculations about the animation of the fetus are now empty of all probative force. (I say this, because there remains among some Anglican Christians a curious belief that this question can be settled simply on the basis of Christian tradition.) This is not to subordinate theology *in principle* to science. Rather, it is to point out that such theological speculations were always *empirical in intent*, lacking only the investigative resources to reach accurate conclusions. And to say that these pre-modern discussions have no probative force is not to say that they have no value for our thinking on the question. They have great *critical* value, in that they expose and refute the philosophical pressures which, then as now, exercise an improper *a priori* influence on what ought to be empirical judgments.

To sum up. The scientific evidence about the development of the unborn child does not prove that the unborn child is a person, because that cannot in principle be proved. We cannot accept any equation of personhood with brain-activity, genotype, implantation, or whatever—for that is to reduce personhood, which is known only in personal engagement, to a function of some observable criteria. However, what the scientific evidence does is to clarify for us the lines of objective continuity and discontinuity, so that we can identify with greater accuracy the 'beginning' of any individual human existence. It is, of course, a purely 'biological' beginning that biology discloses to us; how could it be otherwise? In adopting it as the sufficient ground of respect for the human being, we are not declaring that personhood is merely biological. We are, rather, exploring the presuppositions of personal commitment. The only ground we have for risking commitment in the first encounters with the new human being is biological "appearance".

One of the most potent philosophical ingredients from which the giddy modern cocktail of technological materialism is mixed is the idealist distrust of appearances. It has, of course, become almost customary in these days to proclaim emancipation from a "Cartesian" body-soul dualism, and there can be few intellectual evils which have not been attributed to this source by someone or other. For the most part, however, the emancipation has proved to be an empty boast. The very least that would be implied by it would be a willingness to get a hold on human appearances once again. It would imply that we stopped treating the bodily manifestations of humanity, its genetic and physiological structures, as though we had entirely seen through them and knew that there was nothing there. It would imply that we stopped talking and acting as though we shared some secret knowledge about a real humanity that was disclosed apart from physical appearances. It would imply that we stopped throwing up specious oppositions between "personalist" and "biologistic" conceptions of the human being. It is true, as we have emphasized, that the human person resists exhaustive analysis, that it has its root in the mystery of divine vocation whereby God confers our individual existence upon us as he calls us by our names. But to that secret calling there is no public audio-link. We know another person by his unfolding manifestation through appearances, and we know him to be something more than the sum of the appearances only as we attend with seriousness to what the appearances manifest. The Samaritan, who proved to be the Jew's neighbour, was the one traveller upon that road who reckoned that he could trust the evidence of his eyes: 'When he saw him, he had compassion.'

Appendix

7

An Introduction to the History and Present State of the Law relating to Abortion in England

C. FRADD

Under English law abortion has always been a crime. Originally the common law seems to have treated it as a form of homicide. The greatest of our medieval jurists Henry de Bracton, one of King Henry III's judges, in his immense and authoritative treatise "De Legibus et Consuetudinibus Angliae" compiled in about the year 1250, wrote, "Si sit aliquis qui mulierem pregnantem percusserit vel ei venenum dederit, per quod fecerit abortivum, si puerperium iam formatum vel animatum fuerit, et maxime si animatum, facit homicidium".[1] (If one strikes a pregnant woman or gives her poison in order to procure an abortion, if the fetus is already formed or quickened, especially if it is quickened, he commits homicide.) The word "homicidium" at that period covered both murder and manslaughter, the word murder (murdrum) being confined to a killing carried out in secret (clam perpetratur).

Exactly when abortion ceased to be treated by the common law as a variety of homicide is not clear. By the early seventeenth century Sir Edward Coke (Attorney-General under Elizabeth I and successively Chief Justice of the Court of Common Pleas and of the Court of King's Bench under James I) whose writings on English law have traditionally been regarded as highly authoritative, wrote, "If a woman be quick with child and by a potion or otherwise killeth it in her womb; or if a man beat her whereby the child dieth in her body and she is delivered of a dead child, this is a great misprision and no murder."[2] Misprision, in this sense, means a high misdemeanour. Other authors, after the Restoration, such as Hale and Hawkins, wrote similarly of the matter.

Sir William Blackstone, the first Vinerian Professor of English Law, one of the judges of the Court of Common Pleas in George III's reign, a renowned jurist whose "Commentaries on the Laws of England" published in 1765 were the most distinguished (indeed almost the only) attempt since Bracton to present the whole compass of English law in an elementary and orderly manner comprehensible to non-lawyers, summarized the history and current state of the law on the subject thus: "Life is the immediate gift of God, a right inherent by nature in every individual; and it begins in contemplation of law as soon as an infant is able to stir in the mother's womb. For if a woman is quick with child, and, by a potion or otherwise, killeth it in her womb; or if any one beat her, whereby the child dieth in her body, and she is delivered of a dead child; this, though not murder, was by the antient law homicide or manslaughter. But the modern law doth not look upon this offence in quite so atrocious a light, but merely as a heinous misdemeanor."[3] Elsewhere he says, "To kill a child in its mother's womb, is now no murder, but a great misprision."[4]

This is the last word we hear of the common law crime, though it may perhaps still exist, for soon afterwards statutes on the subject begin to appear. The important point to note is that abortion was always criminal at common law. The analysis of the nature of the crime changed over the centuries, but under one head or another abortion has always been illegal.

The first statute on the subject was that known as Lord Ellenborough's Act passed in 1803. This Act, passed partly in response to pressure from the medical profession, strengthened the law. Previously, as has been seen, abortion was a misdemeanour, but by this Act it was made a felony without benefit of clergy, and thus punishable by death. (Professor Edward Christian, the first Downing Professor of the Laws of England, in his edition of Blackstone's Commentaries published in 1809, draws a parallel between this and the Jewish law on the subject.[5]) The Act applied when any noxious or destructive substance was wilfully and maliciously administered to any woman quick with child. The same Act provided that where any medicine should be so administered or any instrument or other means used to cause an abortion and the woman should not be or should not be proved to be quick with child then the offenders should be guilty of felony and liable to be fined, imprisoned, set in the pillory, whipped or transported for up to 14 years. The Act stiffened the law. It may also have been intended to clarify it, but if so it failed. The distinction between women who were quick and those who were not or were not proved to be quick was found awkward in practice and was abandoned when the law was recast in 1839.

The Offences against the Person Act, 1839 established the law in substantially its modern form. It was re-enacted with only slight alterations in the Offences against the Person Act, 1861 which is the statute which governs the matter today. It provides by s.58 as follows:

> Every Woman, being with Child, who, with Intent to procure her own Miscarriage, shall unlawfully administer to herself any Poison or other noxious Thing, or shall unlawfully use any Instrument or other Means whatsoever with the like Intent, and whosoever, with Intent to procure the Miscarriage of any Woman, whether she be or be not with Child, shall unlawfully administer to her or cause to be taken by her any Poison or other noxious Thing, or shall unlawfully use any Instrument or other Means whatsoever with the like Intent, shall be guilty of Felony, and being convicted thereof shall be liable, at the Discretion of the Court, to be kept in Penal Servitude for Life ...

The distinction between felonies and misdemeanours has in recent years been abolished, but the punishment for this crime remains anything up to life imprisonment.

By s.59 of the 1861 Act it is an offence punishable by up to three years' imprisonment to supply or procure poisons or instruments knowingly for the purpose of abortion.

An oddity of the English common law was that while it was murder to kill anyone who had been born and a misdemeanour to kill a child while still in the womb, it was no crime at all to kill a child while in the actual process of being born. To remedy this defect the Infant Life (Preservation) Act, 1929 was passed. The first section reads as follows:-

> 1. (1) Subject as hereinafter in this subsection provided, any person who, with intent to destroy the life of a child capable of being born alive, by any wilful act causes a child to die before it has an existence independent of its mother, shall be guilty of felony, to wit, of child destruction, and shall be liable on conviction thereof on indictment to penal servitude for life:
>
> Provided that no person shall be found guilty of an offence under this section unless it is proved that the act which caused the death of the child was not done in good faith for the purpose only of preserving the life of the mother.
>
> (2) For the purposes of this Act, evidence that a woman had at any material time been pregnant for a period of twenty-eight weeks or more shall be prima facie proof that she was at that time pregnant of a child capable of being born alive.

It will be seen that this does not deal only with the child while in the process of being born. Bills on this subject introduced in 1908 and 1927 had used the phrase "during the birth thereof", but the final version now enacted extends to any time before the child "has an existence independent of its mother". Furthermore it gives protection to any child "capable of being born alive". Obviously this stage is reached a long time before the child starts being delivered and therefore this statute overlaps the field covered by the 1861 Act.

Thus the result of the legislation so far was that by 1839 at the latest all deliberate abortion was felonious and by 1929 so also was killing a child in the process of being born unless to preserve the mother's life.

This state of affairs was resented by many in the changed moral climate after the Great War. Partly from a desire to make the welfare of the mother the paramount consideration regardless of the life of the child, but largely from motives of pure personal convenience, pressure developed for the relaxation of the abortion laws. The mode of attack upon the old view was by an insistent clamour upon the theme of the awful choice which sometimes arose, or was thought to arise, between saving the life of the mother and the life of the child. The crucial moral distinction between deliberate killing and inevitable death from natural causes came to be obscured or ignored. It is possible to see the proviso (set out above) to s. 1(1) of the 1929 Act as the first fruit of the new view, although that was not the object of the statute.

There was no majority in Parliament for a relaxation of the law, but the Courts proved amenable to "progressive" opinion. In the case of *R.* v. *Bourne* [1939] 1 K.B. 687 the evidence given was that a girl of 14 years had become pregnant after being violently raped by a number of soldiers. Dr Bourne, a leading obstetrician, who later regretted his part in the affair, carried out an abortion with the consent of the girl's parents, on the grounds that the continuance of the pregnancy might cause the girl serious injury. The doctor was prosecuted for carrying out an illegal abortion contrary to s. 58 of the Offences against the Person Act, 1861. At the trial Mr Justice MacNaughten seemed determined not only to encourage the jury to acquit Dr Bourne but also to make a statement of the law which would permit many abortions in the future notwithstanding the clear statutes to the contrary. In his direction to the jury he stated, without any authority, that the proviso (quoted above) to s. 1(1) of the 1929 Act (permitting an abortion to save the mother's life) must be read into the 1861 Act, and then went on to indicate that in his view there was no essential difference between a danger to the life of a mother and a danger to her health. By this means he led the jury to believe that conduct which was acknowledged to be in contravention of the clear words of a criminal statute was, nevertheless, not illegal.

The legal analysis that this direction to the jury has received has represented it as an example of the defence of necessity, which is one of the general defences to crime, but ordinarily a highly restricted one. It rests upon an implied assumption of an omission by Parliament to provide a defence. "Circumstances occurred which rendered it necessary to break the law. If Parlia-

ment had thought of these particular circumstances it would not
have made the conduct criminal", is what the accused relying on
such a defence is effectively driven to say. Obviously it would
quickly undermine the authority of Parliament and obedience to
the law, not just with regard to abortion but in respect of all
crimes, if the defence of necessity were generally accepted. It
was, therefore, highly unsatisfactory that the Rule in *R.* v.
Bourne should ever have formed part of the law of England, both
because it placed the law relating to abortion upon a highly
dubious footing and because it constituted a dangerous extension
of the doctrine of necessity.

Unfortunately the repeal of the Rule in *Bourne's* case came
only with the Abortion Act 1967 which replaced the evil of that
Rule with the much worse evil of permitting doctors to carry out
abortions in a wide range of cases. The Rule is repealed by s. 5 (2)
of the Act which states, "For the purposes of the law relating to
abortion, anything done with intent to procure the miscarriage of
a woman is unlawfully done unless authorised by section 1 of this
Act." Section 1 of the Act reads as follows:-

1. (1) Subject to the provisions of this section, a person shall
not be guilty of an offence under the law relating to abortion
when a pregnancy is terminated by a registered medical
practitioner if two registered medical practitioners are of
the opinion, formed in good faith—

(a) that the continuance of the pregnancy would involve
risk to the life of the pregnant woman, or of injury to the
physical or mental health of the pregnant woman or any
existing children of her family, greater than if the
pregnancy were terminated; or

(b) that there is a substantial risk that if the child were
born it would suffer from such physical or mental abnormalities as to be seriously handicapped.

(2) In determining whether the continuance of a pregnancy
would involve such risk of injury to health as is mentioned
in paragraph (a) of subsection (1) of this section, account
may be taken of the pregnant woman's actual or reasonably
foreseeable environment.

(3) Except as provided by subsection (4) of this section, any
treatment for the termination of pregnancy must be carried
out in a hospital vested in the Minister of Health or the

Secretary of State under the National Health Service Acts, or in a place for the time being approved for the purposes of this section by the said Minister or the Secretary of State. (4) Subsection (3) of this section, and so much of subsection (1) as relates to the opinion of two registered medical practitioners, shall not apply to the termination of a pregnancy by a registered medical practitioner in a case where he is of the opinion, formed in good faith, that the termination is immediately necessary to save the life or to prevent grave permanent injury to the physical or mental health of the pregnant woman.

Sections 2 and 4 will be mentioned later and section 3 is irrelevant to this essay. Section 5 not only by subsection (2) repeals the Rule in *Bourne's* case but also by subsection (1) expressly preserves the Infant Life (Preservation) Act, 1929. Sections 6 and 7 deal with certain definitions and formalities.

It will be seen that the Act does not replace the law which preceded it. It does not codify the law on the subject of abortion. It does not even repeal or amend a single word of the earlier statutory provisions—sections 58 and 59 of the Offences against the Person Act, 1861 and the Infant Life (Preservation) Act, 1929—which remain in force. The Abortion Act is grafted on to the old law and has to be read as one with it. For example, s. 5 (2) (quoted above) tells us that an abortion is illegal unless authorized by s. 1. It does not specify the nature of the illegality. To ascertain what crime has been committed if an abortion is not authorized by s. 1 it is necessary to refer back to the 1861 and 1929 Acts which create the relevant crimes and remain the governing statutes.

As the Abortion Act has not replaced the previous law on the subject, neither has it legalized abortion. It does not say that an abortion shall be legal in such and such circumstances. It is wholly negative in form. It exonerates participants in an abortion operation from prosecution in certain circumstances. Abortion remains illegal, but those people in those circumstances are exculpated. This is not accidental. It springs from the second of the two motives which lay behind the Act—not just to facilitate abortion but also to drive out "back street abortionists". The most effective way of accomplishing this was to re-assert that all abortion was to remain illegal unless authorized. The result is that all abortions are *prima facie* illegal.

The other important point to note about the general scheme of the Act is that it is purely permissive. It permits a doctor to carry out an abortion if the conditions mentioned in s.1 are fulfilled, but it does not oblige a doctor to carry out an abortion even if those conditions are fulfilled. There is a logical corollary to this. This is that no-one has a right to an abortion, for if a woman had such a right it would have to be matched by a corresponding duty on the part of a doctor to provide that to which she had a right, and, as has been seen, the Act imposes no such duty. When people speak, as some are prone to do, of "a woman's right to choose" to have an abortion, they are voicing their own theoretical opinions and are not stating the law of England as it actually stands.

The position, therefore, is that abortion is very far from being lawful in every case. This is not always appreciated. It is commonly assumed, for example, that if qualified doctors give their certificate and the abortion takes place in a hospital or an approved clinic then the abortion is legal. This is very far from being necessarily the case. The nett result of the 1861, 1929 and 1967 Acts is that an abortion is permissible only if:

(a) The child is not capable of being born alive (for otherwise the killing would be an illegal act of child destruction contrary to the 1929 Act) and

(b) It is carried out by a registered medical practitioner; and

(c) It is carried out in a National Health Service hospital or other establishment approved by the Secretary of State for Health and Social Security for the purpose; and

(d) Two registered medical practitioners have formed the opinion in good faith,

Either, that the balance of risk to the woman or her existing children as between termination and continuance of the pregnancy favours termination,

Or, that there is a substantial risk that the child would be born seriously handicapped.

If the doctor carrying out the operation believes that the abortion is immediately necessary to save the mother's life or to prevent grave permanent injury to her health then a second opinion is not required and it does not have to be carried out in a hospital or other approved place. Such cases are, of course, extremely rare.

Abortions have, notoriously, become very common indeed in recent years. This is not because they are all legal, but because it is difficult to prove them to be illegal. There are several reasons for this. First, there is a conspiracy of silence. The woman has wanted the abortion; the doctor has been willing, and often well paid, to carry it out; and the baby, the chief sufferer, does not survive to complain about it. Secondly, a doctor is a respected professional person and it is not easy to convince a jury that he has formed his opinion other than in good faith. Thirdly, the risks as to which an opinion has to be formed are unquantifiable and thus essentially matters of judgment. It is only in the most blatant of cases that the doctor who actually saw the woman at the time can be shewn to have erred in his judgment. For these reasons few prosecutions are brought. Let it be quite clearly understood, though, that this is not because most abortions are legal, but because it is difficult to prove them to be illegal. It is a problem of evidence.

When the conspiracy of silence breaks down then there can indeed be the evidence to support a prosecution. Such a case was *R.* v. *Smith* [1974] 1 All E.R. 376. The doctor had bungled the abortion and the woman became very ill. As a result she was willing to give evidence against him. Her evidence was to the effect that there had been no second opinion, that he had not assessed the risks, and that he had really been interested only in getting the money for his fee—evidence which the jury believed and which led them to convict. In how many countless thousands of other cases must the same essential illegality also be present—no interest whatever in the relative risks, and abortion on request provided the money is forthcoming? Yet because all goes smoothly no evidence of illegality is given, so therefore there are no prosecutions and thus no convictions. The vicious result of this is that the impression builds up in the public mind, and perhaps even in some judicial minds, that a legal abortion is always available if desired. Yet the law says nothing of the sort.

For an abortion to be legal under s.1(1)(a) of the 1967 Act the balance of risk must favour termination. The relevant risks are (i) a risk to the life of the pregnant woman, (ii) a risk to her physical or mental health, and (iii) a risk to the physical or mental health of the existing children of her family. The two doctors must assess the risks honestly according to proper medical practice. They are required to examine the particular woman before them and assess her personal health (or her children's, as the case may be) and not just statistical averages. They must take account of her age and the length of time the pregnancy has already continued. Lord Justice Scarman (as he then was) has pointed out that in forming these opinions "a great social responsibility is firmly placed by the law on the shoulders of the medical profession".[6] The opinions must be formed in good faith and in a trial the question whether or not they have been formed in good faith "is essentially one for the jury to determine on the totality of the evidence . . . By leaving the ultimate question to a jury the law retains its ability to protect society from an abuse of the Act."[7] It is beyond the scope of an essay on the law to give detailed attention to all the medical considerations which should be taken into account when doctors form their opinions, but, to take an example, Lord Justice Scarman quoted with approval the evidence of a doctor in *R.* v. *Smith* that where risk to the mental health of the pregnant woman is relied on (as it was in that case and is in 85% of cases) ". . . one would want to know as much as one could about the patient's general background and so on. . . . Then there is the girl's own history, her past medical history, has there been mental illness in the family, one would expect to check that."[8] The contrast between what the law requires and what commonly occurs these days is too glaring to call for further comment.

The circumstances in which an abortion may be legal have been enumerated already. It is sometimes said that an abortion in the first 13 weeks of pregnancy must always be legal (provided the formalities are observed) because there is always some risk to life or health from a pregnancy and almost no risk from an early abortion. As a statement, this is simply untrue, because there is generally little or no risk from pregnancy to a young mother in good health, while an abortion, even in the first few months, can cause haemorrhage and can lead to subsequent sterility quite apart from the possible emotional disturbance and other mental effects. As an argument, it is fallacious as it does not compare like with like. It compares statistics for maternal mortality among mothers of all ages and in all states of health with those for maternal mortality from first trimester abortions. Almost all such abortions are carried out on young women in good health. There is practically no mortality from pregnancy among young mothers in good health. Deaths from pregnancy, barring accidents, occur only among older women or those with high blood pressure or otherwise in poor health. Thus, if a true comparison is made, statistics do not prove that abortion is safer and therefore do not make early abortions automatically legal. In any case, it is the individual patient whom the doctors must examine and about whom they must form their opinions, not the generality of pregnant women gauged by reference to statistics.

In recent years, since the invention of the post-coital pill sometimes called the "morning after pill", it has been argued that s.58 of the Offences against the Person Act, 1861 does not apply to the fertilized ovum before it becomes implanted in the womb and that therefore the administration of this drug (which is thought to work by preventing implantation) is not an illegal abortion. The present Attorney-General has himself adopted this view on the grounds that "Whatever the state of medical knowledge in the 19th century, the ordinary use of the word 'miscarriage' related to interference at a stage of prenatal development later than implantation."[9] This is, in fact, wrong. All the leading Victorian medico-legal textbooks state that the law against abortion applies from the moment of conception. A good example is Charles Tidy's "Legal Medicine" (London, 1883) in which at p.154 appears the following passage:

> The ovum as really lives from the moment of conception, as does the child or the man. Criminal abortion, therefore, is as criminal at the instant of conception, if we could tell it, as at any other point of pregnancy. The life may be feeble and the embryo incomplete, but neither feebleness of life, nor incompleteness of embryo constitute the slightest argument against the existence and perfection of the vital principle.

It would seem, therefore, that s.58 of the Offences against the Person Act, 1861 does forbid abortion from the very moment of fertilization, as indeed Professor Glanville Williams (when criticizing the law) always maintained that it did.[10] As two doctors cannot possibly give an opinion in good faith that the balance of risk from the continuance of a pregnancy favours termination when they do not even know whether a pregnancy exists to continue, it follows that the act of administering to a woman a post-coital pill or causing her to take such a pill is an illegal procuring of abortion and that the Attorney-General is wrong in his opinion on this point. The view of the law presented here is, after all, what first principles would suggest because the post-coital pill (so far as is known) works not by preventing conception but by preventing the embryonic child already conceived from surviving.

Fertilization in vitro has started to occur in recent years and so-called "test tube babies" have been born. There have been no decided cases on this subject, neither is there any statute governing the matter, and it is thus not known whether the practice of fertilizing in vitro is legal or not.

The position of those who conscientiously object to abortion is dealt with in section 4 of the Abortion Act. By sub-section (1) it is provided that "no person shall be under any duty, whether by contract or by any statutory or other legal requirement, to participate in any treatment authorised by this Act to which he has a conscientious objection." By the word 'treatment' it means, of course, abortions. This provision applies not only to doctors but also to nurses, anaesthetists, radiologists, hospital ancillary workers and indeed everyone concerned. The onus of proof of con-scientious objection rests upon the person claiming it, so it is as well for those who do object to abortion to make this clear to their employers from the outset. The exemption is paramount and no contract of employment or disciplinary regulation can validly detract from it.

The only possible qualification to this is in the case of emergency operations to save the mother's life or to prevent grave permanent injury to her health. It is improbable these days that any such case would occur. If one were to happen, though, sub-section (2) provides that conscientious objection is not to affect any duty to participate in an abortion in such circumstances. It is highly doubtful, however, that there is any such duty. Abortion remains *prima facie* an illegal operation. From the earliest times until 1938, far from there being any duty upon anyone to participate in abortion operations, there was a duty upon everyone not to do so. The idea that there might be at times a duty to abort was invented by Mr Justice MacNaughten in *R.* v. *Bourne*, being a logically inevitable corollary of the defence of necessity enunciated by him in his direction to the jury to secure Dr Bourne's acquittal. With the repeal of the Rule in Bourne's case by s.5(2) of the Abortion Act itself any duty there might ever have been to abort in any circumstances whatsoever must have gone too. Thus s.4(2) attempting to restrict the scope of conscientious objection must, because of the way it is phrased, consist of words empty of meaning.

The Abortion Act shews that it is a true creature of the modern age not just in its permissiveness but also in its bureaucracy. By virtue of s.2 of the Act no abortion may take place without the completion of two forms—first, a certificate that the two doctors have formed the required opinion as to the risk if the pregnancy continues, and second, a notification by the doctor performing the abortion that he has done so. Failure to comply with the Abortion Regulations (which prescribe these forms) is itself a criminal offence involving a fine of up to £1,000. More importantly, an incomplete or carelessly completed form may itself be evidence of an illegal abortion e.g. if the reasons given for the abortion are not such that any honest doctor could have held the opinion in good faith that the balance of risk favoured an abortion. Sometimes an accurately completed form can be evidence that an abortion which has taken place amounted to an illegal act of child destruction because the pregnancy had lasted long enough for the child to have been capable of being born alive. These forms, however, are not generally available to the police as they are required to be kept confidential by the Department of Health and Social Security.

The law of Wales is the same as the law of England. Nothing in this essay must be assumed to apply to Scotland or Northern Ireland where the law is in many respects different.

1 Selden Society edition, 1968, Vol.II, p.341
2 3 Institutes p.50
3 Book I, p.129
4 Book IV, p.198
5 Exodus 21:22
6 *R.* v. *Smith*, supra at p.378
7 Ibid. at p.381
8 Ibid. at p.382
9 Hansard, 10 May 1983, col.239
10 The Sanctity of Life and the Criminal Law (London, 1958), p.141